SHE

And Other Plays
by
Anthony Clark

Nordville

© 2023 Anthony Clark

ISBN: 978-1-7391030-5-7

First edition
All rights reserved

The rights of Anthony Clark to be identified as the author of this work have been asserted by them in accordance with the Copyright, Designs & Patents Act 1988.

No part of this play may be reproduced or transmitted in any form or by any means without the written permission of Wordville. No performance of any kind may be given unless a license has been obtained. Applications should be made before rehearsals begin. Publication of this play does not necessarily indicate its availability for performance.

All Performing Rights – All rights whatsoever in this play are strictly reserved. Applications for all performances, including readings and excerpts, by professionals or amateurs in the English language should be addressed to The Production Exchange Management, The Exchange, Somerset House, Strand, London WC2R 1LA. office@theproductionexchange.com.

Cover illustration by Nicola Clark

Proofread by Jennifer Sieg

Wordville

www.wordville.net

For Marlene, Jess, Poppy and Maddy.

SHE, comprising seven duologues, was first produced by Theatre Accord in association with The Production Exchange, and first performed at the Tara Theatre, London on 9 February 2023. Then on tour to Cheltenham Everyman, Midlands Arts Centre, The Belgrade Coventry, The Theatre Royal Winchester, Swindon Arts Centre, The Lighthouse Poole, The Merlin Frome, The Phoenix Exeter, The Haymarket Basingstoke, Yvonne Arnaud Theatre, Guildford and the Omnibus in Clapham.

The original cast was as follows:

SHE
Directed by Poppy Sutch
SCARLETT .... Chenise Lynette
CORALIE .... Safeena Ladha

NUNKHEAD
Directed by Poppy Sutch
MARLENE .... Chenise Lynette
JESS .... Safeena Ladha

LOVERS
Directed by Maddy Corner
LOVER ONE .... Chenise Lynette
LOVER TWO .... Safeena Ladha

WARRIORS FOR HUMANITY
Directed by Antony Clark
RUTH .... Safeena Ladha
SAM .... Chenise Lynette

MOTHER'S FRIENDS
Directed by Maddy Corner
TASHA .... Safeena Ladha
ELEANOR .... Chenise Lynette

WIDOWS
Directed by Maddy Corner
PEARL .... Chenise Lynette
RUBY .... Safeena Ladha

CHILDISHNESS AND MERE OBLIVION
Directed by Poppy Sutch
EDIE .... Chenise Lynette
MARY .... Safeena Ladha

All plays designed by .... Jessica Curtis
Lighting by .... Ros Chase
Sound by .... Grace Clare
Production Stage Manager .... Ewen Roberts
Deputy Stage Manager .... Kirsty White
Music for song and poster design .... Nicola Clark

CAST

SAFEENA LADHA
Playing: *Coralie, Jess, Lover 2, Ruth, Tasha, Pearl, Safeena*

Safeena trained at University of Gloucestershire and The Centre - Performing Arts College, graduating in 2020. Most recently, she played Daisy Buchanan in *The Great Gatsby* (Immersive Everywhere). Other theatre credits include Stick Lady Love in *Stick Man Live* (Leicester Square Theatre), Cassandra, Andromache and Menelaus in *Troilus and Cressida* (Edinburgh Fringe Festival), *Coriolanus* (Rose Theatre Bankside) and *Into the Blue* (Edinburgh Fringe Festival). Commercial credits include: Ocado, Clearscore sponsors Married at First Sight Australia. Dance credits include *Conform to Rebel* (Redbridge Drama Centre), *Hard to Love* by Bexx (music video). Choreography credits include *Hard to Love* by Bexx (music video).

CHENISE LYNETTE
Playing: *Scarlett, Marlene, Lover 1, Sam, Eleanor, Ruby, Chinese*

Chenise has just completed her BA (Acting) at Mountview Academy of Theatre Arts in which she played roles such as #00 in *The Wolves* and Harriet in *The Man of Mode*. This is her first professional engagement.

CREATIVES

ANTHONY CLARK
Writer and Artistic Director of Theatre Accord.

Previously Artistic Director of Hampstead Theatre (2003-10), Associate Artistic Director Birmingham Rep (1990-2002), Artistic Director Contact Theatre (1984-90) and Assistant Director Orange Tree (1981-83). He has freelanced extensively working with companies that include The National, RSC, Young Vic, Bristol Old Vic Leicester Haymarket, Nottingham Playhouse and Tara Theatre. His plays include. *Paradise of the Assassins* (Theatre Accord National Tour), *Our Brother David* (Watford Palace) *The Power of Darkness* trans Tolstoy (The Orange Tree), *Wake* (The Orange Tree), *Tide Mark* (RSC), *Green* (Contact Theatre). He has written several adaptations for children including the multi award-winning *The Red Balloon* (Contact, BOV, Olivier Theatre NT).

POPPY SUTCH
Co-Director

Poppy graduated from the MA Directing Course at Drama Centre, Central Saint Martins. Whilst there, she assisted professional directors Owen Horsely, Michelle Chadwick, Donnacadh O'Briain and Harry Burton. Her own directing credits include Jack Thorne's *Mydidae* and the premiere of Liam Borrett's *As I have Loved*, for the Platform Studio. As a writer and film maker she wishes to tell and share female led stories. She has written for the VAULT Women's Writes Fest in 2019 and written and directed an original short film *Harper* which won best short film at Fuse Film Festival and was a finalist at the Ealing Film Festival. After *SHE*, Poppy is directing a new film in Ireland, *Tigh na Sióg*.

MADDY CORNER
Co-Director

Maddy graduated from the MA Directing Course, Central Saint Martins. She has assisted directors Kane Husbands, Kate Bannister, Toby Clarke and Owen Horsley. Her directing credits as a student include new plays *Trade* by Ella Dorman-Gajic and *Sima* by Ellen Bannerman. She produced *Trade* at the Omnibus Theatre in Clapham and on tour in the UK in 2022, supported by Arts Council England. She led the devising process and directed two verbatim shows *Mother [singular]*, based on the lives of single mothers in Lambeth at Platform Southwark 2018, and *She.* exploring what it means to identify as female with students from Croydon High, which went to the Edinburgh Festival 2019. Maddy directed *Brainstorm* by Company Three at Edinburgh Fringe 2022. Recently, Maddy has been working at The Traverse, Edinburgh on new play *Kill the Second Coming with Slime and Pies* by Ellen Bannerman and is directing *The Interview* by Eleanor Roberts at the Blue Elephant. She is an Alumni Mentor at The BRIT School.

JESSICA CURTIS
Designer

Jess trained at Motley. Recent work includes *Vincent River* (The Bridge Theatre, Brussels), *A Postcard From Morocco* (Dutch National Opera Academy), *Jekyll And Hyde* (Derby) *Brief Encounter* (Stephen Joseph Theatre), *Genesis Inc.* (Hampstead Theatre), *Loosing Venice* (The Orange Tree Theatre), **Uncle Vanya** (The Almeida), *Villette, Dangerous Corner* (West Yorkshire Playhouse), *Pod, Provok'd* (devised at Guildhall School of Music & Drama),

Kiss Me Quickstep, Haunting Julia, Love Letters (The Queen's Theatre, Hornchurch), *One For The Road, Glass Cage, Follies* (Royal And Derngate, Northampton), *The Holy Rosenbergs* (National Theatre), *Hotel Cerise* (Theatre Royal, Stratford East), *Another Door Closed* (Theatre Royal Bath), *Endgame* (Liverpool Everyman), *Dangerous Corner* (West Yorkshire Playhouse and West End), *Frankenstein* (Frantic Assembly, Northampton), *Burial at Thebes* (Nottingham Playhouse/Barbican/US Tour) and *Rhapsody, Fantasy* (Royal Ballet At The Royal Opera House).

Jessica has also designed the Grosvenor Park Open Air Season 2013-2016/2021, the opening season at Storyhouse and bar interiors for Underbelly at the South Bank, Hyde Park and Leicester Square. She is part of the Society of British Theatre's sustainability working group.

ROS CHASE
Lighting Designer

Ros is in her final year of training on the Theatre Technology course at Guildhall School of Music & Drama (graduating in 2023). She is interested in theatre as a form of education, inspiration and amplification for the voices of underrepresented communities, especially women and members of the LGBTQ+ community. Ros' work has been described as 'a masterclass in how to light a small space' by WhatsOnStage and she was nominated for Best Lighting Design of a new play or musical by Broadway World UK in 2022. Her recent credits include *For a Palestinian* at Camden People's Theatre and Bristol Old Vic; *Rapture* at the Pleasance Theatre; *Shake the City* at the Leeds Playhouse and Greenwich Theatre; *TuckShop's Dick Whittington* at the Phoenix Theatre; *In the Heat of That Night* at the Space Theatre; *Cinderella* at the Hounslow Arts Centre; and *Hyde & Seek* in the Milton Court Theatre at Guildhall.

GRACE CLARE
Sound Designer

Grace is a recent graduate of Backstage Academy with an MA in Live Event Design, where she specialised in Sound. She also has a BA (Hons) in Stage Management and Technical Theatre from the Royal Welsh College of Music and Drama. Her credits while training include *Wife* (Richard Burton Theatre, Cardiff), *The Writer*, Sherman Studio, Cardiff). *Twelfth Night Remembered*, (The Bute Theatre, Cardiff. Remote release). She has also worked as a designer on commissions for exhibit installations. Recent Credits include *Bubbles* (Studio 1, Production Park) and *Perception*, (Trinity Walk,

Wakefield). Alongside her technical work, Grace also designed the sound for *The Fish Cage*, (Alma Theatre, Bristol and Rondo Theatre, Bath).

EWEN ROBERTS
Touring Production Manager

Ewen recently graduated from London Academy of Music and Dramatic Art where he studied Production and Technical Arts. Since graduating he has undertaken a variety of roles and has been involved in projects at the Hampstead Theatre, The National Theatre and has enjoyed touring across the UK.

KIRSTY WHITE
Deputy Stage Manager

Kirsty is a freelance Stage Manager who trained in Theatre Production at the University of Winchester. She worked on various projects throughout 2022, including *Father Christmas* at the Lyric Hammersmith, *Nine Night* at the Leeds Playhouse, the Birmingham Commonwealth Games Opening and Closing Ceremonies and Southampton Pride's Main Stage.

THEATRE ACCORD

Theatre Accord is a small to midscale touring company, founded in 2016 based in Frome, Somerset. It aims to inspire and support creative people, to enjoy and use the medium of theatre to understand their differences and celebrate what they have in common.

TheatreAccord@gmail.com

THE PRODUCTION EXCHANGE

The Production Exchange [TPE] is nearing its tenth birthday. During its first decade it has been busy delivering the organisation's charitable mission: to support early-career practitioners in the creative arts. It does this by providing development opportunities, professional management, mentoring services and pastoral support to early-career practitioners to empower them and help them to develop the necessary skills to become the next generation of creative artists. The charity has a broad Artistic Policy informed only by the ability of all pieces of work to illuminate the condition of humanity in contemporary society. The work is channelled through two distinct, though complementary, fields of activity.

The Production Company specialises in new writing development and subsequent production.

Over the past decade, TPE has produced and managed more than 50 projects of different sizes. From the first reading of a new play to the full production and touring of a number of works. The company believes that there is no substitute for learning on the job and it is always excited to help in any way it can—encouraging anyone who wants to start the ball rolling, to make contact. The first consultation is always free.

The Artist Management looks after Actors, Writers, Directors and Musical Directors, with a vast array of other creatives. Clients' work spans every area of the industry from the smallest theatre above a pub to a big Hollywood studio. The philosophy is simple: to be represented by TPE you must be brilliant at what you do. The company's fundamental belief is that it needs to represent the widest cross section of the society in which it is situated. In order to be true to that belief, the aim is to develop a client base that reflects the world in which we live. As part of that push for truly authentic and legitimate representation, TPE has a specific focus in representing artists from the D/deaf and the LGBTQ+ communities.

www.theproductionexchange.com

1. SHE 1
2. NUNKHEAD 20
3. LOVERS 36
4. WARRIORS FOR HUMANITY 46
5. MOTHER'S FRIENDS 58
6. WIDOWED 70
7. CHILDISHNESS AND MERE OBLIVION 75

A play for 2-14 actors in 7 Scenes. An interval should be taken after Scene 3. All the character are in their 20s apart from Lover 1 & 2 who could be younger.

SHE
Scarlett
Coralie

NUNKHEAD
Marlene
Jess

LOVERS
Lover 1
Lover 2

WARRIORS FOR HUMANITY
Ruth
Sam

MOTHER's FRIENDS
Tasha
Eleanor

WIDOWED
Ruby
Pearl

CHILDISHNESS AND MERE OBLIVION
Edie
Mary

<u>SHE</u>

A messy room in a small flat, in a new build in a rural town. All the characters mentioned are from this town. SCARLETT (20s), dishevelled, in food-stained, ill-fitting nightwear, is sorting and folding a large pile of baby clothes from a plastic laundry basket.

CORALIE (20s), smartly dressed in a coat, stands away from SCARLETT. She has a suitcase with her. 'SHE' (3 months) is crying in the room next door. Under the cries, the distant tinkle of a musical mobile playing 'Relaxing Music for Your Baby'.

SCARLETT: You're late.

CORALIE: Rush hour.

SCARLETT: Four, you said.

CORALIE: I would have phoned, but—

SCARLETT: You were driving.

CORALIE: Got a charger I could borrow?

SCARLETT: Somewhere.

CORALIE: *(Taking off her coat)* You wouldn't happen to know where, would you?

SCARLETT shrugs. Beat.

SCARLETT: What's with the case?

CORALIE: I didn't want to leave it in the car.

SCARLETT: Thought it might get stolen.

CORALIE: *(Placing the case to one side)* It's Rob's.

Beat.

CORALIE: *(Referring to her coat)* Where can I put this where it won't be in the way?

SCARLETT: *(No answer)*

CORALIE traces her finger through the dust on a chair and hangs her coat on the back.

CORALIE: Where did you say that charger was?

SCARLETT: I didn't.

CORALIE: Do you know?

SCARLETT: I'll look for it in a minute.

CORALIE: Thanks. Is there anything I can do?

Rob's planned a City Break. I don't know where. He's going to surprise me. To celebrate our 'three-years-of-being-a-couple.'

SCARLETT: Okay.

Pause.

CORALIE: I could do with a holiday. Spring is our busiest time. When everybody who's been thinking about moving starts the process.

SCARLETT: Why are you here?

CORALIE: I thought, as a kind older sister, I'd come and see how you were.

SCARLETT: We're fine.

CORALIE: How's she doing?

SCARLETT: Fine.

CORALIE: It's been weeks.

They listen to the baby crying.

Is she alright?

SCARLETT: She's fine.

CORALIE: She doesn't sound fine.

SCARLETT: She's fine.

Beat.

You said you'd be here at four.

CORALIE: I would have been here earlier but on Fridays the lads leave me to man the place on my own. It's not fair. I'm always there for the clients. I do more visits and sell twice as many properties as any of them. I hate myself for being so... so... compliant. Four years I've been there, and still feel I have something to prove. Why?

SCARLETT: You're a woman.

CORALIE: Will you start again?

SCARLETT: Start what?

CORALIE: Work.

SCARLETT: Don't be stupid.

CORALIE: Employers are far more accommodating, you know. These days they have to be.

SCARLETT: I've never had a job for more than a month.

Pause.

CORALIE: Scarlett?

SCARLETT: *(Still folding the laundry)* Coralie?

CORALIE: Scarlett?

SCARLETT: That's my name.

CORALIE: I can't see why you didn't tell me.

SCARLETT: What?

CORALIE: Why can't you just be honest with me?

SCARLETT: About what?

CORALIE: About... you know...

SCARLETT: About what?! Is that why you've come? To accuse me of something I didn't do till I feel I've done it? You're always doing that. It was you that dropped the iron out of the window not me.

CORALIE: That was ages ago.

SCARLETT: When we were kids, I got the blame for all your shit.

Beat.

CORALIE: You said you'd never have children. The world being the way it is, you said 'it wouldn't be fair'. Why'd you change your mind?

SCARLETT: You said, 'it would distract me from myself and make me feel better.'

CORALIE: Now wait a minute? You're saying I said, 'having a baby—would—

SCARLETT: 'Would distract me from myself and make me feel better.' Yes.

CORALIE: When?

SCARLETT: You know when.

Pause.

CORALIE: You can't remember, can you? Because I didn't.

SCARLETT: You did.

CORALIE: Never. Not me. Someone else.

Beat.

I'll be honest with you... as honest with you as I hope you'll be with me...I may have thought, but I never said—I may have thought to focus on somebody other than yourself would relieve your anxiety, but I never said—

SCARLETT: I don't feel any different.

CORALIE: Worse?

SCARLETT: (*No answer*)

CORALIE: You're feeling worse and it's my fault. Your problem, Scarlett, is you've always got to find someone, or something to blame for what's gone, going wrong in your life. As far as I'm concerned you knew what you were doing.

Silence.

SCARLETT: Some days she must shit half her bodyweight.

CORALIE Any chance of a cuppa tea?

SCARLETT: If there is any.

CORALIE: Do you want me to go out and get you some?

SCARLETT: No.

CORALIE: Juice?

SCARLETT: Juice?

CORALIE Water then?

SCARLETT: Help yourself. It's in the jug with the charcoal.

CORALIE goes into the kitchen.

CORALIE: Has 'she' got a name, yet?

SCARLETT: I've got a year.

CORALIE: *(Off)* What do you mean?

SCARLETT: Before she has to be registered.

CORALIE: (O*ff*) A year? So, for the time being she's still 'She', then?

SCARLETT: She is.

CORALIE: *(Off)* Have you tried any names?

SCARLETT: *(No answer)*

CORALIE: *(Off)* You know, I always thought I'd be a mother before you.

CORALIE comes back into the room.

CORALIE: For the first three months babies are supposed to look like their Dads so they don't do a runner. Who does she remind you of?

Pause.

Scarlett?

SCARLETT: Coralie?

Beat.

CORALIE: I know it's difficult for you. I know your 'persistent depressive disorder' or 'apocalyptic anxiety' or whatever they now call whatever it is you've got, tires you out, causes forgetfulness and sometimes you behave irrationally but I don't believe you didn't know what you were doing.

SCARLETT: When?

CORALIE: Then.

SCARLETT: When's then?

CORALIE: And I don't believe you didn't know now who you were doing it with.

SCARLETT: I don't know what you're talking about.

CORALIE: Didn't you have to register the father's name on the birth certificate?

SCARLETT: No.

CORALIE: But you could have done? Why didn't you?

SCARLETT: *(Shrugs)*

CORALIE: I wasn't aware you had a—none of us were—let alone you were getting enough to lose track.

SCARLETT: It happens.

CORALIE: My last birthday, who were you shagging?

Beat.

SCARLETT: She gets through a lot of baby-grows in a day.

Pause.

CORALIE: I don't like to think of you doing this on your own.

SCARLETT: What?

CORALIE: Bringing up a child.

SCARLETT: You think I'm a bad mother, don't you?

Beat.

CORALIE: I can't remember what she looks like. Let me go and say, 'good night.'

SCARLETT: No.

CORALIE: Why not? She's still awake.

SCARLETT: We have our routine.

CORALIE: You let her cry herself to sleep?

SCARLETT: So?

CORALIE: But when it's been going on and on, don't you worry? You worry about most things.

SCARLETT: They said, 'you'll never get time to yourself if you don't establish a routine.'

CORALIE listens to the crying while SCARLETT folds the clean laundry.

CORALIE: I'm curious to see how she's changed.

SCARLETT: Are you?

CORALIE: At this age they change so fast.

SCARLETT: Do they?

CORALIE: Shit, Scarlett, this flat stinks. If you won't open the windows, you should get some air fresheners.

SCARLETT: They're toxic.

CORALIE: I don't know why you don't use disposables.

SCARLETT: Because eight million a week end up as landfill.

CORALIE: Yes, but—

SCARLETT: Or they're burnt.

CORALIE: What's wrong with that?

SCARLETT: Greenhouse gases! Global warming. Planet extinction.

CORALIE: I don't know, it seems everything invented to make life easier is bad for it. You don't have to torture yourself or 'She' for the sake of the planet. If we're really threatened with extinction the human race will find a way. If it's easier to use disposables, I say, use them.

SCARLETT: *(Suddenly upset)* But when nothing seems to make a difference it's difficult to know what to do.

CORALIE: Don't start. Stop it. Stop it. Now! Stop crying! It's bloody difficult but you've got to trust human resilience. Stop crying.

SCARLETT: *(Crying)* There's a climate emergency and the earth's on the brink of extinction and you don't give a fuck. All you ever think about is you!

CORALIE: STOP CRYING! That's not true.

SCARLETT: You think I'm a bad mother.

CORALIE: Stop it! Stop crying!

SCARLETT tries to control her upset.

Have you taken your medication?

SCARLETT: Yes.

CORALIE: Have you?

SCARLETT: Yes.

CORALIE: When was your last assessment?

SCARLETT: *(Recovering and continuing to fold the clothes)* I'm alright.

CORALIE: I remember the last time I was here, she was lying in front of the fire, diagonally across my favourite cushion. That close to the heat, I thought she'd burn.

SCARLETT: That's why you've come, isn't it? You think I'm a bad mother. You think I can't cope.

CORALIE: Mum made that cushion for me, you know. Yours was the one with the panda paws. Mine was the one with the ladybirds.

SCARLETT: Mine was the one with ladybirds, yours had paws. Little panda paws, not spots. I'm surprised you don't remember.

CORALIE: Where is it?

SCARLETT: What?

CORALIE: My cushion.

SCARLETT: My cushion's in there.

CORALIE: I want it back.

SCARLETT: It's not yours.

CORALIE: It is.

SCARLETT: Why?

CORALIE: Because I don't want you taking anymore of what's mine.

SCARLETT: I've never taken anything of yours.

Pause.

CORALIE: I went to pull her away from the fire. And you said, 'don't you dare.'

SCARLETT: I'd just got her off to sleep.

CORALIE: She can't have been more than a couple of weeks.

They listen to the crying.

SCARLETT: Have you come to take her away?

CORALIE: When did she last feed?

SCARLETT: When she was hungry.

CORALIE: She had enough?

SCARLETT: Yes.

CORALIE: And you don't think she's still hungry?

SCARLETT: No.

Pause.

CORALIE: I brought you a present.

CORALIE opens the case and hands SCARLETT a present. SCARLETT opens it. It's a new baby grow.

CORALIE: From Rob.

Beat.

SCARLETT: Robert?

CORALIE: My fiancé.

SCARLETT: I know who Robert is.

CORALIE: Then what's with the Robert? It's Rob. His Mum bought it for him, to give to me, to give to you.

SCARLETT: So, it's from her.

CORALIE: Yes, I suppose so. From him, from her.

SCARLETT: It's pink.

CORALIE: For a girl.

SCARLETT: Why does everyone have to gender stereotype the whole time?

CORALIE: Why can't you be grateful for once in your life? She means well.

SCARLETT: Wearing pink will affect her prospects.

CORALIE: She's a baby.

SCARLETT: Look what's happened to you.

CORALIE: What do you mean? I like pink.

SCARLETT: Precisely and that's why they take advantage of you at Drivells, because you've let them define you. And that starts with wearing pink as the only option if you're a girl.

CORALIE: You're being ridiculous. It wasn't the only option. I happen to like pink. You didn't.

SCARLETT: She doesn't need any more pink clothes.

CORALIE: All right, I'll get him to ask her to change it.

Pause.

SCARLETT: Can you buy shoes in different sizes to make a pair?

CORALIE: As soon as she falls asleep... I'm going to sneak in and have a look, and if I find my cushion, I'm taking it back.

SCARLETT: One pair where one shoe is bigger or smaller than the other, can you?

CORALIE: I don't know. It's ages before she starts walking. Ask the health visitor. They still coming?

SCARLETT: *(No answer)*

CORALIE: Are they? Scarlett? They are still keeping an eye on you?

SCARLETT: Yes.

CORALIE: She's being checked? Regularly? Why won't you let me see her?

SCARLETT: I don't want you to wake her up.

CORALIE: But she isn't asleep.

SCARLETT: But when she's asleep, I don't want you waking her up.

CORALIE: But she isn't?

SCARLETT: She'll never settle if you go in there.

CORALIE: But I want to see my niece.

Pause. CORALIE sits.

CORALIE: Were you jealous?

SCARLETT: Of what?

CORALIE: Me.

SCARLETT: *(Ironic)* 'Always', according to you.

SCARLETT stops folding.

CORALIE: How are your nipples?

SCARLETT: What?

CORALIE: The myxomatosis?

SCARLETT: What?

CORALIE: Whatever it's called.

SCARLETT: Myxomatosis is a rabbit disease. It blinds them. Mastitis.

CORALIE: Still on the antibiotics?

SCARLETT: They don't work anymore. When she sucks. It's like needles.

CORALIE: Why don't you stop, and feed her formula?

SCARLETT: And mess up her kidneys?

CORALIE: What?

SCARLETT: Melamine.

CORALIE: What are you talking about?

SCARLETT: Three hundred babies got sick and fifty-four died.

CORALIE: Where did you hear that? When?

SCARLETT: In China.

CORALIE: What?

SCARLETT: It was in the baby milk.

CORALIE: China's not 'here.'

SCARLETT: I had to throw the telly in the bath.

CORALIE: Scarlett, you're mad.

SCARLETT: If you can't unfuck it, chuck it.

CORALIE: What?

SCARLETT: I'd rather torture my tits than 'She' lose a kidney.

CORALIE: But if she can't breastfeed what else are you supposed to do?

SCARLETT: Who says she can't? She can. When she wants to.

CORALIE: Are you sure she's not hungry?

SCARLETT: She always cries at bedtime.

CORALIE: What if she's in pain?

SCARLETT: You think I'm a bad mother, don't you?

CORALIE: I'm saying I think it's time one of us went to her.

SCARLETT: No.

CORALIE: Please just let me pick her up. Let me rock her. Wind her. Sing her a lullaby.

SCARLETT: She'll stop.

CORALIE: I could do what cousin Pam does and drive her 'round the block'? She swears the purr of the engine is the only way of getting Jasmin to sleep.

SCARLETT: Stop worrying. I'm the one that worries not you.

Pause.

CORALIE: What colour are her eyes?

SCARLETT: Her eyes? Blue.

CORALIE: What colour were his eyes?

SCARLETT: Whose eyes?

CORALIE: Oh, come on Scarlett, you must remember the colour of his eyes. Her father's eyes. Were they brown?

SCARLETT: All babies start with blue eyes.

CORALIE: That's a myth.

SCARLETT: If you know why are you asking?

CORALIE: Why won't you tell me the truth? I'm her aunt.

SCARLETT: I'm her mother.

CORALIE: Then act like one.

They listen to the crying.

CORALIE: Is it colic? Does she suffer from—Have you got any—what was it Mum used to give us? Began with a 'G.'

Gripe water? Have you got any? Would you like me to go to the chemist for you?

SCARLETT: No.

CORALIE: I'm going to phone a doctor.

SCARLETT: Your battery's flat.

CORALIE: I'll use yours.

SCARLETT: It's lost.

CORALIE makes towards 'She's room.

SCARLETT: You're not going in there!

CORALIE: I need your charger.

SCARLETT: No.

CORALIE: I'll be quiet.

SCARLETT: You won't see to find it.

CORALIE: I'll turn the light on.

SCARLETT: No, you won't.

CORALIE: I'll leave the door open.

SCARLETT: You bloody won't.

Silence.

CORALIE: You know, if you can't cope you can always ask them to take her away... before someone makes the decision for you.

SCARLETT: I've not changed in the way you thought I would, have I?

Pause.

CORALIE: If you could kill anyone in the world to make this world a better place who would it be? I won't tell anyone. I'd kill... I think you know.

SCARLETT: Me.

CORALIE: You first.

SCARLETT: Kill me then.

CORALIE: I didn't mean you'd be the first person I would like to kill. I meant you go first.

Kill... Anyone... If you had the opportunity to kill someone to make this world a better place, who would it be? Politician? Parent? Sibling? Lover? Child?

SCARLETT: Piss off and leave me alone.

Pause.

CORALIE: Not until you tell me whether she still looks like her Dad?

SCARLETT: You know, I don't know who that is.

CORALIE: You do. I know you do. Why won't you admit it?

SCARLETT: I don't.

Beat.

CORALIE: I know.

SCARLETT: You don't.

CORALIE: He told me.

SCARLETT: Robert?

CORALIE: See! You do know. You bloody know. All along you bloody knew and you wouldn't—

SCARLETT: Because it was your idea.

CORALIE: What was?

SCARLETT: 'She' was all your idea.

CORALIE: What?

SCARLETT: Robert told me.

CORALIE: What kind of a sister fucks their older sister's fiancé at her birthday party?

SCARLETT: He told me you asked him to.

CORALIE: What kind of older sister asks her fiancé to do that?

SCARLETT: You.

CORALIE: You. He told me you asked him to.

SCARLETT: He told me you asked him to. You.

CORALIE: I never.

SCARLETT: I never.

CORALIE: Rob and I agreed that if we were going to marry there'd be no secrets between us, and so last week we were out celebrating our first meeting, he'd had a bottle of wine or two when he goes very quiet and says, 'there's something you should know...' And then he comes out with it—that at my birthday party you got loose as a goose and when I'd gone to bed begged him to... um—that you told him, I had said, that I thought you needed... that I thought it would be good for your well-being and I really didn't mind, and so he did what you wanted him to do. And honestly it wasn't because he loved you, but because he loved me...

And I felt the blood stream from my face—I said 'Go! Go! I never want to see—just go! How could you? How could she?!' And then he started crying like a baby 'Sorry. I'm so sorry'...over and over again. 'I'll make it up to you, Coralie. We'll go on a city break.' And that's when I left. What the hell were you doing, Scarlett?

Beat.

What kind of sister screws their older sister's fiancé? Tell me! On my bloody birthday? Tell me! In the same bloody house? Tell me!

Beat.

SCARLETT: You'd gone to bed, and he was following you up, and I was puffing up the cushions on the couch, when he turned back and stopped me and whispered that you told him you knew it wasn't my birthday, but you thought I deserved a present for being such a kind sister, and you'd asked him to give it to me just as soon as you were asleep.

CORALIE: He said what?

SCARLETT: He said that you and Mum and he had discussed it. Something I needed that you knew I'd like, that'd make all the difference to my life, and he couldn't wait to give it to me. I told him, well, if that's the case he should go to bed and give it to me in the morning, when everybody could share my pleasure in receiving whatever it was.

CORALIE: Did you know what he was talking about?

SCARLETT: He left and came back a little later. I was half asleep when I heard him walk past... toward the kitchen, open the fridge and help himself to another beer and something else I don't know what, I could smell it on his fingers. His silhouette was swaying in the light. And then he came and sat... He patted the blanket and scraped the hair off my face... muttering something about how beautiful I was, everybody thought so, but what a shame it was that I didn't... He said, what a shame it was that I was so scared of the world, and his present would 'make all the difference.' And then he asked if he could give it to me now, and I said, 'No.' I said, 'there's nothing that couldn't wait till morning.' But he took no notice and got closer.

CORALIE: You're lying to me.

SCARLETT: And I told him, 'Go back to bed.' You were waiting for him and he should be ashamed of himself and then in this creepy gentle voice, 'honestly, you'll love it, everyone's agreed it's what you need.'

CORALIE: You're lying to me.

SCARLETT: And then he slipped his hand under the blanket. It was so hot I froze. And then he... he...

Whispered in my ear, that I smelt nice... that I felt nice...

CORALIE: What are you talking about! You're lying. Shut up, Scarlett! SHUT UP!

SCARLETT: I'm not lying. He caressed my mouth with his stinking fingers, and when I bit one, he slipped the other between my gum and lip and pulled so hard I thought he'd tear the skin. He said he'd hurt me some more if I tried anything, and then he rolled me onto my front with the other hand, and then half on and half off the cushions... I had one knee on the rug, he pulled my pants high up, and then down. I thought I was going to die, Coralie.

CORALIE: Oh God, I never... we never... why—why didn't you scream for help? We were—why didn't you do something? Why didn't you tell me? Scarlett you might have—

SCARLETT: How could I after you gave him permission.

CORALIE: Don't be ridiculous! How could you believe?!! I'd never—I wouldn't. How could you ever think I'd do such a thing?

SCARLETT: He said, if I didn't like the present, and dared to tell you so, he'd tell you it was all my fault for flirting, begging and daring him to do it.

CORALIE: I don't know what you're talking about.

SCARLETT: I told him—

CORALIE: Why didn't you tell the police?

SCARLETT: I told him I would, and he said, with my mental history, no one would believe me.

Beat.

CORALIE: You're right. Why should I believe you?

SCARLETT: When did he tell you he was her father?

CORALIE: I told you. Last week.

SCARLETT: What did he say?

CORALIE: That you asked him to.

SCARLETT: I never.

CORALIE: Neither did I.

Beat.

SCARLETT: *(Upset)* If I wasn't your younger sister, none of this would have happened.

CORALIE goes to touch her sister.

SHE starts crying again. CORALIE waits. SHE stops crying. SCARLETT returns.

CORALIE: Why should I believe you?

SCARLETT: I never wanted a baby.

CORALIE: Two days ago he came to Drivells white as a sheet and said he hadn't slept since he'd told me, and why wasn't I answering his calls, and then he said that he'd told his mother the whole story and she said that I should ask you to get a DNA test done on the baby, and if it was his baby, he should have custody.

SCARLETT: *(Bites her lip and nods her head slowly).*

CORALIE: You know what a Mummy's boy he is. She told him she'd brought him up to take responsibility for stuff, and she didn't want her granddaughter, if that's who 'She' is, being brought up by someone with your mental health, and neither should he. And perhaps he could persuade me to ask you if you wouldn't mind if I looked after her.

Silence.

CORALIE: I could pretend she was mine for you, Scarlett. If that's what you would like... Scarlett?

Pause. SHE starts crying again.

SCARLETT goes to SHE's room. CORALIE starts packing the case with baby clothes. After a while SHE stops crying. SCARLETT returns with the ladybird cushion mentioned earlier.

SCARLETT: *(Offering CORALIE the cushion)* Here! She's sleeping if you want to go and have a look. I've left the light on.

CORALIE goes into the room. SCARLETT looks at the bedroom door.

THE END

<u>NUNKHEAD</u>

A French restaurant dining room in a small town. MARLENE (20s), a partner in a successful interior design company is waiting to have a meal with her old school friend JESS (20s). JESS is doing a PhD in Crop Science.

MARLENE: *(To the audience)* I phoned to book a table this morning, and Nunkhead—Ash to her sycophants, short for Ashanti because she smoked too much—can't have recognised my voice, said, 'sure, it's a Monday, just turn up.'

Nunkhead, which is the female version of lunkhead, which means stupid man, apparently, changed her tune when she saw me. 'We're fully booked,' she announced, tucking a tea towel in her apron. No, hint of an apology. No, 'Oh hello, Marlene, long time no see.' No, 'I'm sorry for bullying you at school. How can I make it up to you now?' Just a feeble excuse about how the online booking system hadn't been working and the council had called Monsieur Fabian, that's her boss, and reserved the whole restaurant for a visiting Delegation of Mongolian Horse Traders. She said the Mongolians were from Ulaanbaatar, and Ulaanbaatar is twinned with Leeds, which is the nearest city to where we are now. She said, Monsieur Fabian said, 'for the sake of international relations it was important not to let the horsemen down.' You know, when someone can't meet your eye, it's because they're lying. So, I asked her, since I remembered how she could never spell 'occasion' at school, to spell Ulaanbaatar.

And she looked at me and then to my amazement got all five 'a's in the right place. 'Look,' I said, 'it's Jess Kharti's birthday.' She flinched at the mention of Jess's name. 'You must remember Jess. I promised to treat her to a meal here tonight. We could go to the pub, but the ambiance isn't a patch on this place, nor the food as good. And, not only is it Jess's birthday, but we're both leaving tomorrow forever.' 'I'm busy. It's going to be the busiest night since I've been here,' she said.

I don't believe you could bully people for four years the way she bullied us, and not feel... feel guilty, some remorse... even if you were a narcissistic sociopath like Nunkhead. I reminded her of how she'd once stuck bubble-gum in Jess's hair during a Maths lesson, and her Mum, Mrs Kharti, had had to hack it out with a Stanley knife and poor Jess looked like she had alopecia for weeks.

'There's nothing I can do,' she said. 'The place is booked out.' 'Okay. When are they due?' I asked. 'Who?' she said. 'The Mongolians? I said. 'Eight,' she said. 'Oh, great, it's only just gone six, we'll be done by then. Jess'll be here any minute. She's never late.' 'It's only me on tonight, and I need a couple of hours to prepare,' she protested. 'Would you like some help?' I said. The thought of ruining her table settings coursed through my veins, and I was hot with vengeful joy. 'No,' she said emphatically. 'You can take that table over,' she said. 'What? The one between the Gents and the disabled toilet?' I squeaked. 'Are you sure? And if the Mongolians don't all turn up? Or cancel?' 'They won't.' She sucked her teeth.

'Thanks, Ash. Oh, and I'd like a bottle of Prosecco, for Jess, immediately. And, by the way, do you know you've got a bogey, the size of a spider's egg-sack in your right nostril?' She pressed the tea towel against her nose. 'Oh, don't do that Ash—not with a tea towel. Ugh!! That's disgusting, Nunkhead.'

Time passes.

MARLENE hums. Glasses and a half empty bottle of Prosecco on the table. JESS arrives in a hurry.

JESS: Sorry I'm late.

MARLENE: What time do you call this? *(Pouring the remains of the bottle for JESS)* Get that down you. Well? Did she recognise you?

JESS: Of course.

MARLENE: Though she pretended not to. We said six. It's nearly seven. What kept you?

JESS: You don't want to know.

MARLENE: I tried calling but it went straight to answerphone.

JESS: What's that smell? Why are we sitting here? It stinks.

MARLENE: The place has been booked out by a party of Mongolian Horse Traders. Guests of the Council and Chairman of the British Horse Society. Jess are you alright?

JESS: I'm fine.

MARLENE: You look a bit puffy round the eyes.

Beat.

JESS: The smell of ammonia is making me cry. Let's move!

MARLENE: Go on then. As long as we're done by eight, which we will be, I can't see there being a problem.

They move to another table or move their table.

JESS: Here?

MARLENE: Great. I told the stupid cunt! I didn't say 'cunt.' I may have thought it, but I didn't say it, because ever since you told me to, I've been embracing the positive power of the word. I whole-heartedly accept, I do, that the word is only an insult if you think strong women with sexual desire are a bad thing, and we don't, do we? I told her it was your birthday.

JESS: Oh shit. Oh no. It's your birthday. It's not my birthday. It's your birthday, isn't it? Happy birthday, Marlene. I completely forgot. I'm so sorry. I've had one of those days. I meant to get you a present. But I didn't. I'm a shit friend. I'm going to get another bottle. On me.

MARLENE: On the house, if everything goes according to plan.

JESS: *(Calling)* Service!

MARLENE: Reparations for a damaged childhood. Nunkhead!

JESS: How much have you had? She must still be feeding the baby.

MARLENE: She's what?

JESS: I'll be straight back.

JESS leaves. Lights dip.

Time passes.

MARLENE: *(Sings - tipsy)*

Today is my birthday.
Today's about me.
The child I once was.
The woman I'll be.

I'll never feel happy,
Till I've overcome
The shame of being bullied
When I was so young.

Lights up. JESS returns with another bottle and a couple of menus.

JESS: It seems while we've been amassing qualifications, Nunkhead's been popping babies.

MARLENE: There's a surprise.

JESS: Two and one on the way.

MARLENE: Who's the Dad?

JESS: I didn't ask.

MARLENE: I doubt she knows.

JESS: Bitch.

MARLENE: *(About the bottle)* Oh, that's better. That's really cold.

JESS: I'll never forget what she did to you that time.

MARLENE: Which time? The time with the bin?

JESS: When she got Robert, Yogesh and... who was it? She was in the year above...

MARLENE: Kadeena.

JESS: What was Kadeena doing getting involved with Nunkhead? I really liked her.

MARLENE: She made them tip the bin on me and, when I wouldn't hand over my phone, threatened to set fire to the rubbish with a purple plastic lighter she'd nicked off... Creepity Creep.

JESS: Mr Candy.

MARLENE: Old letch! And when I adamantly refused, they lit the paper and polystyrene and I thought I was going to die—I did, honestly—

JESS: I know you did. I'd have been terrified. I'm terrified for you just thinking about it.

MARLENE: It was like a funeral pyre. I was on the brink of being burnt alive like French Joan.

JESS: Joan of Arc.

MARLENE: That's the one.

JESS: One of the greatest feminists ever.

MARLENE: When I started to shriek, Nunkhead suddenly panicked and asked the others to stamp out the flames, but they didn't want to ruin their trainers, so the boys pissed on me.

JESS: You should have called the police.

MARLENE: They stole my phone.

JESS: Afterwards.

MARLENE: You don't though, do you?

JESS: I should've told Ms. Verma.

MARLENE: At that age, you don't though, do you? For fear of what they'll do next. Joan of Arc wasn't a feminist.

JESS: She acted like a man, though, didn't she?

MARLENE: As an instrument of God to restore France to Frenchmen not to empower and save the lives of women.

JESS: *(Looking at the menu)* What's a Croque Monsieur? And what's the difference between that and a Croque Madame?

MARLENE: They're both ham and cheese toasties. One's posh with a sloppy egg on top.

JESS: Monsieur?

MARLENE: Madame.

JESS: Bloody expensive.

MARLENE: Have what you want. We're not paying.

JESS: I feel awful saying this, but back then, I would've loved to have been Nunkhead's best friend.

MARLENE: Wasn't I good enough for you?

JESS: You were better than a best friend.

MARLENE: She was so jealous of the way you looked—

JESS: I was hideous.

MARLENE: You were gorgeous, Jess. And clever.

JESS: Face like a vegetable.

MARLENE: No.

JESS: Ridged and pocked like a gourd.

MARLENE: Talking of zits, do you remember how she used to sit at the back of the class squeezing the blackheads on Rob's neck?

JESS: And he squealed like a piglet.

MARLENE: The reason everyone liked her was because of her Titanic tits and her tight-packed pear-drop arse. She was a mean cow. Look at her silhouette. There. In the door there. They're still huge. Do tits keep growing like old men's ears?

JESS: It's only 'cause she's breast feeding—

MARLENE: Why's she bringing the baby to work?

JESS: She's breast feeding! Or can't afford the care.

MARLENE: She may have been a bully, but she was the first to grow breasts. And back then we were impressed. At least I was. Ready to order?

JESS: What're we doing?

MARLENE: She starts taking the order. We appear to know what we want. And then we change our minds and keep changing them.

JESS: And when we eventually settle on what we're having and the food arrives, we eat it, and then complain it wasn't what we ordered, and therefore we're not paying.

MARLENE: And the wine's crap and the plates aren't clean. And cutlery can't have been put in the washing machine. Hey, I'm a poet!

JESS: That's right, and we'd like to speak to her manager, because she's been as rude as a bear.

MARLENE: What does that mean?

JESS: Abusive.

MARLENE: And when Monsieur Fabian arrives, we say 'S'il vous plait, monsieur manager. We'd like an apology, and a complete refund.'

JESS: If he's like my Dad he'll acknowledge our complaint calmly, believing 'every complaint is an opportunity to learn,' and say he'll see what he can do about the bill—

MARLENE: We say, 'Bill? What bill? We want a complete refund and voucher for another meal. Two vouchers.'

JESS: But we're leaving tomorrow.

MARLENE: For our parents. Four vouchers. And if he says 'no,' we tell him, or I do, how earlier Nunkhead said it'd be fine just to turn up, and then when she recognised me from school, invented some crazy story about a faulty online booking system and Mongolian horsemen.

Then, Monsieur Fabian, faking contrition, will start nodding his head like one of those back-seat car-window dogs, and flicking Nunkhead's thighs with a tea towel behind his back, until she apologises to us, before he sacks her, and offers to buy our silences with chocolate eclairs.

JESS: Yummy!

MARLENE: Mission accomplished. I'm going to tell her we're ready to order.

JESS: I'll go.

MARLENE: I will.

JESS: It's your birthday!

JESS leaves. Lights dip.

Time passes.

MARLENE: (Sings)

Hugging the school walls
Scuffing my feet
Excluded from joining
The in-crowd elite.

Always admitting
But knowing all along
What I did was right when
You said I was wrong.

Drenching my pillow
With unhappy tears
Not wanting to feel
So desperately scared.

I prayed to your God,
My parents and friends
I threatened to bring my
Own life to an end.

Light up. JESS returns.

JESS: She's coming.

MARLENE: She's better hurry up, or we won't have time to eat before the Mongolians.

Pause.

JESS: I don't know, but I've been thinking... By doing this, aren't we... isn't she—

MARLENE: What?

JESS: In so far as she is still controlling us, our emotions and actions... isn't she...

MARLENE: What?

JESS: Still bullying us?

MARLENE: No. She needs to know how much she hurt us. How much life she took from us. Life we'll never get back.

JESS: It just feels... it doesn't matter.

Pause.

MARLENE: So you're on the cusp of finishing a PhD on how to extend the life of ... what root is it?

JESS: The tapioca root.

MARLENE: You're brilliant. I bet in five years you'll be awarded the Nobel Prize for staving off famine in the Sahara.

JESS: In Mexico, Marlene. That baby's not happy. It's a staple diet in Southern America not Africa.

MARLENE: And you're about to marry a gorgeous, serious, empathetic young Romanian—

JESS: Argentinian. Not anymore.

MARLENE: Argentinian who knows more about the restorative qualities of blue whale sperm than anyone else on the planet. How are preparations going for the great day?

Pause.

JESS: They're not.

MARLENE: What?

Pause.

Jess?

JESS: I don't want to talk about it.

MARLENE: Honestly you two. Who was it this time?

JESS: Not me.

MARLENE: He'll be back.

JESS: No he won't.

MARLENE: But you're perfect for each other. Ambitious, active, your families get on well... I mean, shit, I thought you were buying a house together.

JESS: Not anymore.

MARLENE: Why?

JESS: I don't know.

MARLENE: Is it marriage he can't cope with? The fact that it was a leap year and you proposed to him? You know, you don't have to get married when there's the trust between you.

JESS: There isn't.

MARLENE: Don't tell me he's been—bloody men.

JESS: I don't want to talk about it. *(Calling the direction of the kitchen)* Ashanti! ASH!

MARLENE: He'll be back. Nunkhead!

JESS: He's left the country.

MARLENE: Where to?

JESS: Romania.

MARLENE: I thought he was Argentinian?

JESS: He is Argentinian, but he's gone to Romania. He was always going to Romania this month. I told you. To give a paper on the restorative powers of whale sperm.

Pause.

MARLENE: When you're ready to talk it through, you know I'll always be here for you. I think she's making us wait on purpose.

JESS: I wonder if she knows you're now a partner in a successful interior design company.

MARLENE: Who has just won the contract to reinvent—

JESS: You got it? You got the Zip Zone contract? My God, Marlene! That's brilliant! Well done!!! Hug?

MARLENE: Hug?

JESS: Come on proper hug!

They hug.

JESS: When did you hear?

MARLENE: This afternoon. We're not called Zip Zone anymore. We've rebranded. We're called Zone.

JESS: Zone?

MARLENE: Just Zone.

JESS: What's happened to the Zip?

MARLENE: Undone. Pure and simple. Zone alone.

JESS: That's brilliant. But why not Zip?

MARLENE: It is brilliant, we're brilliant! Nunkhead's not and we are!

Beat.

JESS: We should pity her. She's the one life's leaving behind when we're the ones getting out of here.

MARLENE: She's ignoring us. Nunkhead!

JESS: Perhaps she's feeling remorseful.

MARLENE: Nunkhead, if you want us out before the Mongolians arrive, you'd better shift your arse tartare over here! Let's move. She'll find it hard to keep ignoring us if we sit in her eye-line.

They move to another table closer to the audience.

JESS: Did you ever wonder how she could afford so many clothes? I mean her family wasn't rich, was it? Her Dad was sweeping chimneys when he wasn't in the pub, and her Mum worked in the chemists. She lived with her Mum, didn't she?

MARLENE: I once saw her clothes-shopping with Mr Candy. It wouldn't surprise me if he was pimping her.

JESS: At school?

MARLENE: I remember you said, on Wednesday afternoons, he locked the art room for life-drawing and made his favourites undress to model.

JESS: It was rumoured.

MARLENE: No smoke without fire.

JESS: Ashanti was one of them, wasn't she?

MARLENE: Definitely. I never told you this, but I was in his photography club... and he used that cupboard on the third floor as a dark room... that's where he tried it on with me. To this day I only have to smell acetate and—today they'd have him arrested and registered.

JESS: If he wasn't dead, you could still report him.

MARLENE: But he is dead, and thanks to Creepy Candy I still find intimacy with some men very difficult.

Beat.

JESS: At the moment I believe I'm unlovable.

MARLENE: Don't be ridiculous.

JESS: No, I do. Somehow, I wasn't good enough for Raoul, was I?

MARLENE: Your self-esteem may be on the floor, Jess, but look at the positives... what you've achieved, how gorgeous you are—enjoy tonight... buy yourself something nice tomorrow.

JESS: Shut up, Marlene.

ASHANTI (unseen) has arrived.

JESS: Oh, hi Ashanti.

MARLENE: Hi Nunkhead! You start.

JESS: You.

MARLENE: For starters, I'll have—I'll have—

JESS: I'll have—

MARLENE: No alright, you go first.

JESS: No, you first.

MARLENE: I'd like, daily soup.

JESS: Soup of the day.

MARLENE: Which is?

JESS: The tart with green salad for me.

MARLENE: Mushroom? What sort of mushroom?

JESS: You hate mushroom.

MARLENE: No I don't. Shilake?

JESS: You do. You hate soup. Shitake. It's a type of mushroom.

MARLENE: Long and stringy or short and stubby?

JESS: You know Ash, some of the things you did to us—

MARLENE: What are you having?

JESS: Like the time, Ash, you put bubble gum in my hair, and another time you said I uploaded a fake nude and posted on Facebook, because I didn't have a boyfriend? I never. After that I wanted to put my fingers in the wall socket.

MARLENE: Remember when you set fire to me? I'll try the sun-dried tomato tart.

JESS: With gruyere condoms. What you did to us—

MARLENE: Croutons, Jess. Croutons. —has scarred me for life.

JESS: I'll have the soup. You don't eat cheese. Was it that you were scared?

MARLENE: Is it vegan? We were scared. Fucking scared.

JESS: It's French onion. What were you scared of?

MARLENE: Had to be the one in charge.

JESS: Was your desire to be popular because you were totally ignored at home?

MARLENE: I won't have the cheesy condom croutons.

JESS: 'Those to whom evil is done, do evil in return.' Did you feel you had to inflict pain on others so that you would appear strong?

MARLENE: Dead right. *(Reading from the menu)* Crevettes Marie Rose.

JESS: Was everything you were doing a call for attention because you were being ignored by people or perhaps even bullied at home? Crevettes are off, you say.

MARLENE: Jess, stop making excuses for her. I'll have the escargot with garlic and herb butter.

JESS: And I'll have the vegan camembert with the tomato chutney.

MARLENE: Just list everything you did to make our lives hell, and say you're sorry, really sorry.

JESS: What would you feel, if when your kids go to school, they—?

MARLENE: And waive the bill for this meal.

JESS: If they were bullied the way you bullied us?

ASHANTI is gone.

She's gone.

MARLENE: It's my birthday and before we leave, I want to know that she understands—

JESS: She understands, otherwise she wouldn't have walked away.

MARLENE: She must apologise like she means it and compensate us.

JESS: It's not going to work bringing up the past and humiliating her.

MARLENE: I want her to know how we felt.

JESS: But supposing back then she felt worse than us?

MARLENE: *(Incredulous)* Are you okay?

JESS: Look Marlene, the only way we are ever going to get an apology out of her is not to bully her in revenge, but to find out why she thinks she did what she did, and if she now thinks it's wrong to have done those things and is prepared to apologise.

MARLENE: And pay for the meal.

JESS: The anthropologist in me says all behaviour is communication.

MARLENE: You're a geneticist. Where are you going with this?

JESS: We've got to ask ourselves what was she trying to say to the world by bullying us? And why has she now just walked away?

MARLENE: So what you're saying is she had crap in her own life she couldn't deal so she took it out on us. There was no need—

JESS: No, I know—

MARLENE: She should have been sectioned for what she did to me.

JESS: The only way we're ever going to get over this is by accepting that life has a bigger purpose than taking revenge on Ashanti. I'm going to ask her a few questions, see she's okay.

MARLENE: Fuck you, Jess, just because you've split with Raoul doesn't mean you have to ruin my birthday. This was going to be fun.

Time passes.

Lights dim.

MARLENE: (*Sings*)

> The scars still run deep
> The nightmares recur
> Without an apology
> I'm still haunted by her.
> Just say you're sorry,
> Then admit to me

Nothing you said I
Should take personally.

Lights up. The sounds of car doors slamming and people arriving.

MARLENE: Well?

JESS: I did my best to de-escalate the situation.

MARLENE: What situation?

JESS: I said 'sorry'—

MARLENE: For what?

JESS: And then she said 'sorry,' and she wanted me to say 'sorry' to you on her behalf—

MARLENE: She can bloody well say it to my face.

JESS: The Mongolians have arrived.

MARLENE: So? If she wants to say sorry, she can say it to my face!

JESS: She's feeding the baby. I've ordered us a taxi.

MARLENE: When she brings the food. She can say it then.

JESS: Look we've got our 'sorry.' What more do you want?

MARLENE: A fun night out and a free meal.

JESS: We'll find somewhere else to have much more fun. Are you coming?

Beat.

MARLENE: Where are we going?

JESS: There's this great place that Raoul took me to.

MARLENE looks at JESS, then in the direction of ASHANTI, picks up the prosecco and follows JESS off.

THE END

LOVERS

LOVER ONE holding a cell phone. LOVER TWO holding a drink. Both are in the same theatrical space but in different places.

Music playing 'Careless Whisper' by George Michael, barely audible.

LOVER ONE: Love, stop pounding my aching sore heart,
 I can't help it if I've fallen for my
 Best friend's long-term boyfriend Matt Hornby-Paul.

LOVER TWO: *(Sighs)*

LOVER ONE: Shit, what am I supposed to do? I've met
 Matt many times before but never knew
 He felt the way he clearly does about
 The way I look and everything I am...
 He says, 'he can't bear to live without me.'
 —'Staying-in' together, the latest plan.
 I mean, when someone says to you, 'you mean
 More to them than anyone they've ever
 Met before,' it's hard not to feel flattered
 And a bit... you know...

LOVER TWO: *(Sighs)*

LOVER ONE: I'm reeling from the feeling that he finds
 Me so appealing, and I'm squealing 'it's...
 It's so, so, so blazing amazing - CRAZY!'

LOVER TWO: *(Sighs)*

LOVER ONE: So embarrassing but fucktitious too!

LOVER TWO: *(Sharp intake of breath)*

LOVER ONE: Brain I'll go insane if you can't help me
 find the right words to explain to Madeleine
 That it wasn't my fault—but then again—
 No, Matt couldn't really help himself... Look,
 honestly, please understand it wasn't
 planned... just something in the beer tonight...

The handsome hunk of our pubescent dreams
Corporealized while you were buying
Another round of luminous mojitos.
I caught sight of Matt who shrugged and flicked
his floppy fair hair back behind his pierced left ear,
smiled seductively, and blew me a kiss
To me... moi... qui ... si, me, ya!
...which I returned flirtatiously.

LOVER TWO: *(Long sigh)*

LOVER ONE:
We glanced at you, and the length of the queue
When the music changed to a tune we both knew.

Music: The Skints' 'Rub a Dub' in the background.

We waited...
Then neither daring to make the first move
but like opposing magnets drawn together
we found ourselves hot-dancing rub-a-dub
—much, too much, too much crotchy crotch-
pressing and releasing high peptides in
the brain, coursing lust-blood through our veins
swelling the parts we now dared—
dared not to touch. Well DARED!
MUST! THRUST!

It was great!

LOVER TWO: (*Breathless*)

LOVER ONE: I don't know where you went..
You must have left
At the sight of us two trying to catch
mirror-ball stars on the crowded dance floor.

The music stops abruptly.

We didn't leave together, you know that.
We looked everywhere for you... Madeleine.

LOVER TWO: (*Relaxed sigh*)

LOVER ONE: Matt has asked me, 'because he can't,' he says,
ask you. He's far too conscience-stricken to.
To ask 'if you'd mind if we'—he's sorry—

But he's sure you'll understand because you've
Always looked out for him before. And now
He doesn't intend to stop loving you,
And honestly, you'll always be my best,
Best friend, I mean it, I sincerely do.

LOVER TWO: (*Sighs*)

LOVER ONE: He's sorry—we both are—so sorry but
these things happen in life... like the moon shines
At night—crap example—but it's hard to—
because you, Matt and I are such good friends
We can't let love destroy the three of us.

LOVER TWO: (*Sighs*)

LOVER ONE: We three best friends for evermore must be!
But sorry, not a threesome sexually.

LOVER TWO: (Sighs)

LOVER ONE: I can't. No Matt. I can't. Maddy's been my
best friend since we were both at primary school
and got the colours of the rainbow wrong
in that nauseating rainbow song.
We share the same tastes, quite obviously,
And she makes me laugh. She's the sun behind
The clouds when my life seems impossible.
I've said, how much her friendship means to me,
To both of us, to you and me and her...
Though I've said it once I'll say it again.
Seriously we're more than friends us three
I can't imagine what my life would be
like if Madeleine wasn't there, can you?

Can't you stay the thrill of a fantasy?!

LOVER TWO: (*Sighs*)

LOVER ONE: Why me? Why now, Matt? So suddenly?
I'm—

LOVER TWO: (*Sighs*)

LOVER ONE: Not as beautiful, as funny, or wise.
And I don't support your politics or
Who you want to be. In every way you're
the wrong type—incompatible with me...

LOVER TWO: (*Sighs*)

LOVER ONE: But I want you, I want you, I want to
wrap you, to wrap me,
    to wrap each other
under the stars, legs and arms,
                                      Kissing
The face off you and swallowing your breath
Till we both melt in the sweltering heat
of our groping desire.

LOVER TWO: (*Sighs*)

LOVER ONE: (*Going for her phone*)
Oh shit, what do I? What do I text?

'Darling Matt go away...' 'No, sweet Matty
Darling stay...' 'Hey gorgeous, I want to be
Your hope until the end of time' Yukee!
'I know you're vulnerable, misguided
And insecure and I can help you find
yourself and we can grow together
Seamlessly, entwined like soft satin sheets
Between our naked bodies, on the bed, the floor
Up against the frosted bathroom door.'

LOVER TWO: (*Sighs*)

LOVER ONE: Oh fuck it, piss off, how dare you play with
my affections so recklessly when you owe
Everything you've got to my best friend.

The phone pings a text message.

(*Reading the text*) 'Hi Rose, it's me Maddy—'

Oh shit, oh hell! 'I'm sorry!'

(Reading on) 'I'm sorry I never said
Goodnight, but I met someone at the bar
Who has made me feel so differently
About everything and everyone... and
As my best friend would you mind telling Matt,
I plan to separate and hire a van
And clear out of his flat as fast as I can.'
(Texting) 'Hi Matty, still awake?
It's me your Rose.'
Oh shit, he's bound to be upset, when I
Have to tell him of her infidelity
the way men are when we leave them despite
The many times they've betrayed us before.
Magnanimous Madeleine has agreed
That we can get together you and me.

(Continuing to text) 'Matt, it's me. We're free to be—'

LOVER TWO: (*Sighs*)

The Music changes to Bob Marley's 'Is this love,' barely audible.

LOVER TWO: What is happening to me...?
In your company...?
I'm a bit tiddly...
I'm showing you my wrists
And fiddling with my clothes
And nodding in agreement
At everything you say...
And liking what you do.
Although what is it, you do?
Precisely?
'No don't tell me.'
'Nothing.'
'Oh God, that's amazing!'
I'm twirling my hair,
Shit, so girly-girl,
What am I doing?
What are you doing to me?
Putting my leg up on the chair,
Tucking my foot under the cushion

Resting my chin on my knee
Honestly not knowing why
I want you to look at
The inside of my thigh.
And suddenly we're sharing
The last bit of pizza.
I start munching your end
You mine.
I mean,
You start munching mine
I start munching yours
You yours, I mine
That's what I mean.
Munch, munch.

LOVER ONE: (*Sighs*)

LOVER TWO: And as we get closer
Your hot breath mists my glasses,
And we're just about to press
Molten mozzarella
in a lip kiss
When you prise my mouth
open with your tongue
And swallow mine.

LOVER ONE: (*Sighs*)

LOVER TWO: I'm gagging.
Let go!
Free.
Giggling.
'That was good.' Yeah, that was good'
'So good'
'Pizza food'
'GOOD'
'Drink?'
'Yeah!'
I catch sight of us both
The back of your head and my face
Cheeks flushed with the night
In the oval mirror

Above the fireplace.
Crrrrrk—
Its mahogany-frame-crust splits
And the curves morph into your arms
And you're holding out a hand to me—
'Coming! I'm coming.'
Hug me hunk!

LOVER ONE: (*Sighs*)

LOVER TWO: You're running me through a field
Of wild scented *masculinia perspirus*
In soft focus slow motion
And the rustling leaves in the trees
Whisper romantic melodies
Which you simultaneously
Are translating for me.
Then we stop...
'Drop!'
And you're kneading
My fleshy bits.

'Stop tickling'
Then pinching
'Oiw!'
Then fingering—
I'm giggling
'Not so fast'
Pressing.

'I've got hiccoughs'

Then you lift me to my feet
And rush me to the woods
And we arrive some place
Near a stream
That once upon a time
Was a canoe hut
And there's still a padlock on the door.

So, that's what the sharp key
around your neck was for.

Slits of sunlight
Through the planked walls
Slash our naked bodies
As we stand looking...
All over each other.
As ravishing now
as we might have
Ever looked before.

You are so in my hopes
I can't wait for whatever
Happens next.
With each caress
I feel my back arch
My heartbeat tighten
My breasts lift
And my nipples harden.
My touch—and your molest—
'Scratch me'—'Lean over.'
My head in your lap—
Your head in mine—
Rub flat belly time.
Do you mind if-?'
'No. Not at all.'
'Sure?'
'It's safe.'
My energy is on you
And you hard in me
And me,
Suddenly me
Intimately wet.

'Wait?'

'Why?'

'Hey!
What are you doing?
Come back!

What's that?
What?
No.

Why?
No!
Not that.
You can't.
Can't do that!

'Come on? Come on, what? NO!'

Put the phone down.

Who do you want to show?
Your friends?
NO!
Before?
'When before?'

One more?
What?

Show me.

LOVER TWO looks at the phone. Flicking through images.

Shit! You—Them?
When? How?
Without—
Oiw!
Hell bent
Upskirted on the escalator,
Cleaning out the fridge.
On the library ladder,
Fetching off the top shelf
A book I bet you said,
Would mean so much to me,
That you had never even read.
SHIT!

Without—
You went ahead and
Posted in my underwear
Thinking that I wouldn't care.

You've a nerve—
You perv, troll, psycho—

Flatter?

LOVER ONE: Misogynist!

LOVER TWO: It doesn't flatter me!

LOVER ONE: Objectifying my body
 For all to see

LOVER TWO: Don't put me out there
 Like this
 This
 Or, that
 This and that,
 Is <u>you</u> ignoring me!

 For what? For why?

LOVER ONE: Slut shaming?

LOVER TWO: Cat-calling?

LOVER ONE: Revenge Porn?

LOVER TWO: I thought we were both about consent
 That we both knew
 what the bloody word meant

 That every step on the passionate way
 We had to check in with the other and say
 Are you sure about this? Is this okay?
 And then we'd agree on what we would do
 That wasn't about just me or you
 But sexing together, loving as two!

 And now you know
 Where you can go
 You can
 You can

LOVER ONE: *(Mouthed)* Fuck off!

LOVER TWO: *(Mouthed)* Fuck off!

'Fuck off' is bleeped out. Music.

THE END

INTERVAL

WARRIORS FOR HUMANITY

A waiting room. RUTH is waiting to catch her local MP, Johnny Singh. She stands behind a supermarket trolley containing boxes of signatures. She is talking to the faceless voice of bureaucracy/officialdom, a person behind a screen, or on a small CCTV camera, perhaps.

The voice may be represented by sound, which may have the rhythm and tempo of speech, but the words are indecipherable.

Piped Music - a selection Acker Bilk's Greatest Hits including 'Stranger on the Shore' and 'What a Wonderful world' plays throughout the scene.

RUTH: I know, I should've booked—No, it's not a benefit issue—I don't need to see a case worker—No, a phone surgery won't help—I'm Ruth, Ruth Dhaker, Johnny knows me. We tweet—You do? That's good—So you know I'm the regional representative of the Warriors for Humanity—You've already signed our petition? That's fantastic! Listen, I can see there are people waiting, but honestly this'll only take a couple of minutes. If Johnny wouldn't mind having his picture taken beside this trolley, it would boost our local campaign—Not that it isn't already a success (*indicating the trolley*). And the number of signatories here is a fraction of the googleplex of global supporters who've signed online, but we could always do with more—A Googleplex? One followed by a hundred noughts. But don't quote me on that—I know he's a supporter—I mean who wouldn't be? The facts speak for themselves. We are so grateful for all Johnny Singh MP has done to get the government to take seriously the United Nations' call to all countries to hold a referendum, or is it referenda? —A referendum for world peace to save the planet. When one hundred and ninety-three countries are going to be going to their people we can't afford not to—Thank you, I prefer to stand—

You'll agree, it's a simple question all nations are putting to their people: 'Do you see any future in the government investing in the armed forces and war, when the cost to the climate is proving fatal? Yes, or No?' —It's not only that more greenhouse gas is admitted in the manufacturing and use of arms than in the manufacturing and use of anything else, but the consequences of global warming... the rising seas, and the powerful storms, famines and lack of fresh water is making so many regions of the world politically unstable, prompting more conflicts, more mass migration and refugee crises. It's a vicious circle—No, honestly, I prefer to stand.

A 'yes' vote in this country will persuade our respective representatives of whatever political persuasion to come together on the matter. It will. It must—For too long, binary politics has silenced the voice of the majority—The Warriors for Humanity speak for the majority. We do. We want to see 'big community.' We want to subordinate economic activity to human life. Human life as a whole, material and spiritual. It's time for everyone to know what it is to be human, to identify as human—As warriors we believe it to be.... to be... I can't help myself I get a bit overcome when I say it... we believe to be human is to be 'useful'—To be useful to as many people as you can be useful to—Look, I've got to return this trolley by 5:30. Honestly, it won't take a minute, we can use my phone—If you don't mind, I'll stand. Every time I sit, my legs feel they want to walk away. It's a recognised syndrome. It's worse when I'm excited.

(Offering the petition to a member of the audience) Excuse me, if you haven't already signed, please do and pass it on. Thank you.

I know you may have a slightly cynical view about what all the activist, environmental groups have been doing , and are still doing... But by getting people to rethink their relationship with the natural world and question the ethos of big business and banking, their contribution to future generations has already been invaluable, but I'll agree with you, has yet to deliver the killer the punch. Because as the years go by, we've seen it all too often... The organization and discipline of these movements breaks down.

Irreconcilable differences appear between the leaders and their followers, and their influence evaporates.

The difference with the Warriors for Humanity is that we're all leaders—Because we know that everyone is a leader the minute they decide to lead by example. It's really that simple—All of us, share the same goal. And all of us, through a well-structured system of people's assemblies, have been negotiating and will continue to negotiate with all local, national and global authorities for world peace to save the planet.

After a 'Yes' vote all nations of the world will agree a date to decommission their ammunition and lay down arms—Please let it be a gentle Tuesday, it's always been my lucky day— They think it'll take four years for each and every warring faction big and small, in every country, to sort out how they are going to resolve their differences peacefully... whether through consultation, mediation, democracy, the rule of law, and reparations... or a combination of them all. Every country will have to do whatever it takes for the survival of the human race. This time they know they will.

Don't you tingle...? Don't the hairs on the back of our arms stand up to know, if you sign, you're on the right side of history?

Enter SAM, walking purposefully to reception. She appears to be answering questions for the unseen person behind a screen.

SAM: (*To receptionist*) —Sam Cole!

RUTH: Excuse me.

SAM: (*To receptionist*) —SAM COLE—

RUTH: Excuse me.

SAM: (*To receptionist*) —I'm homeless.

RUTH: Excuse me, I was here first.

SAM: (*To receptionist*) —I need help—

RUTH: I'm sorry—

SAM: (*To receptionist*)—And my condition is this government's priority—

RUTH: Would you mind if—

SAM: (*To receptionist*) —I'm not late—

RUTH: They're busy this afternoon. They're running a bit behind. Sorry, you're going to have to wait.

SAM: Fuck your 'sorry', this is my time. (*To receptionist*) What's the point of booking a slot if you won't stick to it?(*To RUTH*) What do you want? I'm next. Sit and wait your turn.

RUTH: I prefer to stand.

SAM: (*Not trusting RUTH*) I know your game!

Pause.

RUTH: Well, perhaps you wouldn't mind Sam if I gate-crashed your meeting with Johnny... it won't take long... couple of minutes just as long as it takes to take a picture of our MP beside this trolley.

SAM: You nick it?

RUTH: No, no I've got an hour to return it.

SAM: I'll take it back for you.

RUTH: That's very kind, but I need to get this petition back to the office to be couriered to Parliament first thing in the morning. I'm Ruth Dhakar, by the way, you may have heard of me. I'm a Warrior for Humanity—

SAM: I was in the army.

RUTH: I'm working to save the planet for future generations.

SAM: I'm looking for job.

RUTH: We're always looking for volunteers.

SAM: Paid.

RUTH: Have you tried the Job Centre?

SAM: They don't want to know me. It was them that said, 'join the army, they're always recruiting' and now I'm unemployable. They tell you loads in the army but not what it's really like. You see your comrades being killed and injured, and you think, 'yeah, I expected that, I can cope with that', but then something tips you.

RUTH: PTSD?

SAM: What would you know?!

RUTH: I watch telly.

SAM: Bastards don't care.

RUTH: I'm sure Johnny Singh will do what he can to contact the services who can help.

SAM: (*To receptionist*) I'm waiting!

RUTH: Won't be long.

SAM: I'm not late.

RUTH: I could never be in the army.

SAM: (*Drinking from a can*) And if your Mum and Dad were never there, brother paralyzed from the neck down and you were doing stuff and doing stuff to pay for what you were doing and having all kinds of shit done to you. Always in trouble. Poor as dirt.

Drifting... in an out of care, then prison, and that's when my probationary officer said, 'try the army.' And I did. And I liked it. My self-esteem shot up and hit the bell. I loved it. I have an 'I love the army' tattoo to prove it. Do you want to see?

RUTH: To tell you the truth tattoos make me feel a bit you know...

SAM: On my thigh. 'Love' spelt in weapons. (*Undoing her trousers*) Have a look. The 'L's a pistol, the 'V's a flick knife, the 'O's a grenade—

RUTH: Thanks, but no thanks.

SAM: The army offered my life structure, regular money and friends, and then it screwed my brain. I've had this bit of medication and that bit of cognitive therapy to rebrain it, but none of it works, I'm still drowning in night sweats, can't concentrate, have roller-coaster moods... and I rage.

RUTH: Have you tried pottery?

SAM: Fuck off.

RUTH: No, I'm serious. They said on this programme that turning a bowl or making a ring mug can work wonders to relieve anxiety.

SAM: Making a mug won't get me a job, or buy me somewhere to live.

RUTH: I'm sure Johnny Singh will make your case to the relevant—Look, you don't mind if I... honestly it won't take long.

SAM: Fuck off! You're not taking my time. I'm fed up with being put to the back of the queue. Wait your fucking turn. (*Shouting at reception*) Does he know I'm here? Sam Cole!

RUTH: I understand your need, but climate change is a real emergency. For the sake of humanity, we all have to arrest what's happening to the climate and let Parliament know we're with the rest of the world. They've got to support the United Nation's initiative, to stop all wars, immediately. You can't afford to put yourself first, Sam, when humanity demands attention.

SAM: War's human nature. And don't call me Sam. We're not friends.

RUTH: Human nature is empathetic and compassionate. I don't know if you know this, but the impulse to help others in times of need is far stronger than to attack them. Love is stronger than hate. Love makes things better, hate doesn't.

SAM: There's always going to be differences of opinion, different ideologies, different beliefs, jealousies.

RUTH: Of course and our road to survival is to incorporate diversity and inclusivity.

SAM: Yeah, well... in the army they said we needed an enemy to know we were right.

RUTH: (*Handing her a Warriors for Humanity brochure*) Here, have one of these. This'll put you right about human nature.

SAM: There's nothing wrong with going to war if the cause is just and people behave properly. And you know that.

RUTH: Name me a war that people remember for good behaviour. I know how hard the army works to dehumanize their recruits to demonise the enemy it's shameful. I'm not blaming you.

SAM: Fuck off. I didn't come here for you to have a 'go.'

RUTH: I am a pacifist and I can't understand why anybody would join the army.

SAM: I told you why. It gave my life a purpose. It was safe. It was exciting.

RUTH: Safe? I bet most of the action you ever saw was interfering in other people's wars. This country's got a terrible reputation for it. You might have felt safe, but whenever we interfere in other people's struggles, I've never felt less safe.

SAM: The army doesn't get to choose 'why' it fights. (*To Reception*) Is anybody going to fucking meet me?

Pause.

RUTH: If you don't mind me asking... What happened?

SAM: When?

RUTH: What was your tipping point?

SAM drinks.

SAM: You really want to know?

RUTH: You don't have to tell if—

SAM: We stopped to search for insurgents in this village... and the captain was bartering fags with the grey beards for information... and I was on top of the Foxtrot chucking jelly babies at the kids, who were jumping up like fish in a pond, trying to catch them in their mouths. We were the peacekeepers, the bearer of gifts, you understand, not the enemy. The peacekeepers who would reinstate their liberties.

RUTH: I'm sorry.

SAM: And there was this little girl, must've been no more than five or six... maybe seven... wearing bangles around her ankles, with little silver bells on them. Like miniature sleigh bells, they were. She was tapping her tambourine and dancing... pounding the dirt with her thin hennaed heels... twisting her supple body with unimaginable joy... those bells... on those bangles… on those dark ankles... glistened in the sun... firing pinpricks of light of joy at us.

Metres away her uncle was stroking his avalanche of a white beard negotiating for more cigarettes when the little girl stepped onto an IED he'd set for us. And BOOM! BOOM it went. BOOM... And she was gone.

RUTH: I'm sorry.

SAM: One minute I'm smiling and clapping, accompanying her and the next I'm scraping her off the windscreen… And when the dust settled... and my eyes cleared—

RUTH: I'm really sorry.

SAM: I found five of her tiny bells buried in the blood-soaked dirt. I flicked the flies and shook the ants off them. I don't know what happened to the rest. She must've had at least ten. In that moment, I guess—Then. That flicked a switch in my brain and nothing the army said to me or did for me could switch it back. My purpose had gone so they let me go, and I started drinking... disgusted... to forget, and couldn't stop, and one thing led to another and now I don't know who I am anymore and seems I've nothing to do... nothing I can do.

V/O: Ms. Cole, we're sorry for the delay. Mr Singh is aware you're waiting. He'll be with you shortly.

SAM: JOHNNY, YOU BASTARD. I HAVEN'T GOT ALL DAY. I'M NOT WAITING. I'M COMING TO GET WHAT THIS GOVERNMENT OWES ME!

RUTH: Shh! Calm down. Calm down. They'll arrest you and then your anger won't have been worth the bother!

SAM: IT'S UNFAIR. IT'S FUCKING UNFAIR. I LOSE MY FREEDOM FIGHTING FOR THE FREEDOM OF OTHERS, AND IT'S SO FUCKING UNFAIR!

RUTH: They'll arrest you and then you'll see how quickly you can put up with their unfairness. You don't want to go back to prison.

V/O: We're sorry we're running a bit late. Please sit and wait in an orderly fashion. Mr Singh knows you're waiting. Sit. We'll have to call security. Sit down!

A security alarm rings.

RUTH: Sit down. Sit down! They want us to wait in an orderly fashion.

They sit.

SAM: (*Still angry, her delivery gaining in speed*) And in an orderly fashion they'll persuade you that they understand, that they're sorry, they'll look into it, they're on your case, but before they do it might be worth you checking the complaints procedures, and cataloguing your facts, and contacting this and that department who will need to talk to this or that department on your behalf who would then have to inform you that, if that were the case, you may be fighting a 'no-cause' cause, and all they can offer you is not what you were expecting but it's all you're going to get. Take it or leave it. I'm not sitting down.

SAM stands.

RUTH: It's a frustrating fact but this world is full of people paid to thwart our anger for no reason other than to protect their own interests. Sit, they'll get to you eventually.

SAM: I'm going to count to three and then I'm coming in, Johnny! One!

RUTH: SIT DOWN! You've got to learn the system to get what you want. If they want us sit, we'd better sit.

SAM: TWO!

RUTH: SIT!

SAM sits.

Did you know, non-violent protests are twice as likely to succeed as armed conflicts?

SAM stands.

SAM: TWO AND A HALF!

RUTH: SIT DOWN! YOU'RE NOT HELPING YOUR CAUSE!

Sam sits. Sam stands.

SAM: I WANT WHAT'S OWED ME! I BOOKED!

RUTH: Go on then! Go on! Don't wait! Go on in there and give Johnny Singh a piece of your mind! Pin him with your story and don't leave until you have what you came for.

SAM: I WILL, I WILL, I'M COMING IN!

V/O: The doors are locked. Security are on the way.

The sound of alarm continues. SAM hesitates and then sits down. The alarm stops.

RUTH: (Sings)

When as a tiny baby
Crying in hunger and pain
Bawling, screaming, wondering why
I was left to cry in vain.
There I learnt my lesson
It's best not to complain
Anger can stress and poison
The logistics of the brain

When fresh-faced I was picked on
By the brutal school bully
The rule was don't retaliate
Sit and suffer silently
There I learnt my lesson
It's best not to complain
Anger can stress and poison
The logistics of the brain

When as a dreamy teenager
Spreading my love about
I felt suicidal to be turned down
Overcome by shame and doubt.
There I learnt my lesson

It's best not to complain
Anger can stress and poison
The logistics of the brain

When I chose what job to do
It had to be worthwhile
Tempted by the offer of a bonus though
I fabricated my profile
There I learnt my lesson
It's best not to complain
Anger can stress and poison
The logistics of the brain

When I'm living comfortably
Free to preach on world affairs
I'll argue I know what to do
From the safety of not being there
There I'll learn my lesson
It's best not to complain
Anger can stress and poison
The logistics of the brain

V/O: To those of you still waiting to see Johnny Singh, I'm afraid his daughter has had a bump in the playground, and he has had to leave immediately. He apologies to all those still waiting. If you'd like to book for next time, you will find the details on line.

SAM: SHIT! Sometimes, I wish the night would wrap me up so tight, I'd never wake up.

SAM hugs herself so tight she starts to rock. RUTH puts the petition down and hugs SAM.

RUTH: (*Sings*)
When I approach retirement
To take stock of my regrets
I hope those missed opportunities
Will be easy to forget.
There I'll learn my lesson
Perhaps I should've complained
Anger and principles both should feed
The logistics of the brain

SAM stares at the petition.

When my mind and body're gone
Absorbed by the shadows on the wall
Let my soul find another life
One fairer than death that's all.
My soul has learned a lesson
It's better to complain
When anger's fuelled by common sense
There's the whole of life to gain.

SAM signs and leaves.

Thank you.

THE END

MOTHER'S FRIENDS

TASHA (20s) and ELEANOR (20s) are sorting old clothes from bin bags, boxes and carrier bags, into a circle of six piles. TASHA has been drinking.

TASHA: Mum's collecting her friends' cast offs to raise money for the hospice. (*Referring to the clothes*) Some of these smell very familiar.

ELEANOR: She won't mind you drinking all her wine, will she?

TASHA: Nah!

ELEANOR: When will she be back?

TASHA: Don't worry, we've got plenty of time. (*Referring to the piles*) Now listen carefully. When we start channelling, the force will push us towards one of these, where you will pick up an item of clothing that encapsulates the spirit's character, and you'll start speaking as them.

ELEANOR: Who?

TASHA: Anybody out there who can advise us what to do with the rest of our lives.

ELEANOR: But if this was a real seance we'd know the names of who we were trying to contact. Wouldn't we?

TASHA: Yeah, well my approach is more egalitarian as 'befits the age.' The state I'm in, I'll take advice from anybody.

ELEANOR: How much have you had to drink?

TASHA: Now step into the centre of the circle, say who you are and explain your predicament.

ELEANOR: And then what?

TASHA: I'll do the same and then we'll wait and see who comes 'a-knockin.' (*Passing her wine*) Here!

ELEANOR: And can we, like, ask them questions, or do they just, like, talk at us?

TASHA: Depends who they are. Just like real life.

ELEANOR: On a real Ouija board though, the spirits would answer specific questions by moving an arrow thing—

TASHA: Planchette.

ELEANOR:—around an alphabet dial. There'd be a connection point between the spirit world and this one.

TASHA: You mean a planchette. My granny was a spiritualist. She had a planchette. The spirit was never in the planchette they were in the person who had their hand on it. The planchette. And they'd spell out the answer with the help of their... their planchette.

ELEANOR: To a specific question. Rah, I can't believe you don't have a game of Scrabble in the house.

TASHA: It'll be fine, these clothes will work a treat.

ELEANOR: Will they, like, answer our questions directly or will we have to, like, guess what they're getting at?

TASHA: What are you talking about?

ELEANOR: Like reading horoscopes. Matching our own experience to like what's there?

TASHA: Fuck knows! Okay, okay! Stand back! (*Stepping carefully backwards out of the circle*) Recap!

ELEANOR: This is mad.

TASHA: This evening we've agreed we're both at a crossroads- Ready?

ELEANOR: (*Nods nervously*)

TASHA: Step into the centre of the circle, Eleanor, and put your life out there. Let's see who's listening.

ELEANOR: (*Stepping forward then pulling back*) You first.

TASHA steps into the circle and finds her karma.

TASHA: (*Staring at the ceiling*) I'm an artist. My name's Natasha Gogh. When I was a student, my art was all about being female, and then I got involved in other activism, digging up other people's stories and making, like, them visible, and now I'm trying to find out who I really am as an artist... in order to make work... work that... I don't know... reveals things about myself that I keep secret... that others will recognise in themselves and be, like, reassured that they are not like alone in this fantastic, wonderful, frustrating, absurd, like, world.

ELEANOR: But her problem is she can't be fucked, oh spirit.

TASHA: I could if I didn't have to work as a part-time carer, a flower arranger, and borrow money off Mum to live... I'd have more time for my art—to think and experiment, and match 'form with content for maximum impact.'

ELEANOR: It's a shame she's got the talent, but not the confidence to explore her own truth, or push herself forward.

TASHA: That's not fair.

ELEANOR: Only an hour ago you said if someone phoned and offered you an exhibition tonight, you'd have to say 'no' because you don't have enough work to show and that you were embarrassed by what you do have.

TASHA: Your turn.

TASHA steps out and helps herself to more wine. ELEANOR steps into the circle.

ELEANOR: Hi, I'm Eleanor, I'm a fashion data analyst. I gather and collate digital information to help retail and fashion companies make loads of money, by predicting trends and consumer behaviour.

TASHA: She's bare good at her job. She's up for a promotion.

ELEANOR: It's between me and one other. A man.

TASHA: She loves the money. There'd be more money.

ELEANOR: But I'm pregnant.

TASHA: And she's worried that if she has the baby she'll miss out on the promotion and the chance won't come again.

ELEANOR: I'm undecided about whether to keep it.

TASHA: For the reason I've just given you, oh spirits, but also because secretly she's worried, she might never conceive again.

ELEANOR: It's not uncommon.

TASHA: That's great, Ellie! That's plenty for the spirits to woo woo on. Okay! Okay? Now the summoning part. And I'm basing this on what I can remember Granny doing when she forgot her Ouija board in Saint Tropez. I haven't done this for a long time.

ELEANOR: If ever.

TASHA: O ye of little faith. Listen carefully and do what I do. Take your Granny and your Mum's date of birth. No, maybe your Mum's and your own would be better—I can't remember Granny's DOB, yours and your Mum should do—my Mum's is 21st October 1966—and then walk round the circle—I'll go clockwise, you (*she turns her finger in an anti-clockwise direction*)—counting the piles you pass as the number of days... so 21 for me...

ELEANOR: Five, for me.

They move at different speed around the circle counting off the piles.

TASHA: You STOP! Stop at that pile and then and walk back in the opposite direction counting piles as the number of months and then stop there, and then walk back the number of years in the opposite direction to the opposite direction you've just walked in, so the same direction you originally walked in, and—

ELEANOR: What? One thousand nine hundred and sixty-six times around the circle?

TASHA: Rah, don't be stupid. The sum of the number.

ELEANOR: You didn't say that.

TASHA: I'm saying it now.

ELEANOR: So, if we're talking 1966, it's one plus nine plus six—

TASHA: Plus six.

ELEANOR: Plus six! Got it. It's twenty-two piles round.

TASHA: Then pick up an article of clothing... and feel the force.

ELEANOR has followed TASHA through the ritual.

ELEANOR: You know this looks like some kind of pentangle. If you start summoning 'she devils,' Tasha, I'm out of here.

TASHA: Shh! Listen, Ellie! Listen!

They listen.

ELEANOR: What am I listening for?

TASHA: Listen!

ELEANOR: (*Whispering*) I'm not interested if it's a man spirit. I'm fed up with Vlad mansplaining and telling me what I should do with my life. You know, I love the father of my child-to-be and, honestly, I wasn't trying to leave him when I said he didn't have to have anything to do with the baby, if he didn't want it.

TASHA: When did you last speak to him?

ELEANOR: Vlad? I'm waiting for him to call me back.

TASHA: Your problem, Ellie, is that you're so frightened you'll make a wrong decision you never make a right one.

ELEANOR: And your problem, Tasha, is you believe decisions make themselves, and you drift from one thing to another and then when things don't turn out the way you want to, you give up.

TASHA: (*Her body suddenly is being pulled in different directions*) On my God, oh my God! Help is on the way! I can feel the force!

ELEANOR: Oh my God, oh my God, babes, are you okay?

TASHA: (*Gyrating weirdly*) Shit! Quick Ellie, feel the flow!

ELEANOR: I can't feel anything.

TASHA: Didn't you hear that?

ELEANOR: What? No.

TASHA: Shh! Whatever you do don't taunt the spirit by asking them when you're going to die. When you're in the zone let the force f-f-f-f-flow.

ELEANOR: Why are you stuttering?

TASHA: Do you know what I m-m-m-mean?

ELEANOR: For fuck's sake, Tasha, you're scaring me.

TASHA: (*Moving backwards and forwards in the circle*) I'm channelling, Ellie. I'm channelling.

ELEANOR: Who is it?

TASHA: Shit! They're gone. You get that sometimes. Spirits dropping in on the wrong seance.

TASHA is suddenly thrust towards a pile of clothes and picks up a knee length skirt in a serious colour, and a white blouse.

MS. YEWTREE (TASHA): 'Coming from a large family I learnt how to negotiate… I know I shouldn't, but do you have any sugar?'

ELEANOR: Excuse me, who are you spirit?

MS. YEWTREE (TASHA): 'Without the law there would be no such thing as society—Butter's not the problem, it's sugar.'

ELEANOR: You probably heard what I want. I don't want to miss out on promotion, the kudos and the extra money but I want to have this child. What would you advise?

MS. YEWTREE (TASHA): 'Thank you—I always loved to argue, and to be paid for it is a real treat. It's not just the money though. I'll have another spoon—'

ELEANOR: Money matters to me, especially in a world where women at my level still get paid less than men for the same job.

MS. YEWTREE (TASHA): 'The focus of all my work is helping others—And one more please!'

ELEANOR: I quite agree, but... you know, sometimes that can be at one's own expense, you know, materially, spiritually and you know, I'm not sure... I'm not sure she can hear me? Can you hear me? (*Pulling the skirt out of TASH's hands*) TASH!

Pause.

TASHA: Shit, I know who that was. I was Ms. Yewtree. One of Mum's closest friends. She has a terrible sweet tooth, and drinks tea by the bucket. (*About the skirt*) She must've worn this.

ELEANOR: I thought spirits had to be dead.

TASHA: She's a brilliant human rights lawyer and very much alive.

ELEANOR: I guess there's no real reason, if whoever is controlling the spirit world has been uploading information about us since we were born, why we shouldn't be able to download spirits past and present.

TASHA: And perhaps future. Wouldn't that be sick if we could meet our future selves? Like in A Christmas Carol where Scrooge sees himself in the future.

ELEANOR picks up a pair of high heels.

ELEANOR: I've always wanted a pair of these. Which one of your mother's friends—?

TASHA: Really?

ELEANOR: (*Starts to shake and run through a number of poses*) Oh my God, here she comes, here she comes!

RITA (ELEANOR): 'It's good grace, it's patience, it's not wearing a smile like a loaded gun. When you've been doing this for as long as I have—I'm not going to tell you how long that is, because it was never a life choice, I fell into it...'

TASHA: Hi, I'm Tasha. Have we met before?

RITA (ELEANOR): 'I'm Rita.'

TASHA: I fell into being an artist because I'm good at art.

RITA (ELEANOR): 'I've fallen into most things... everything really. With long straight legs, no tits and a face like mine, that's what sort of happens to women. Spotted by a scout in Biba, became a model, lost my virginity in his MG—I was earning—not much, but a bit—and I thought that was great until—I'm not going to go there—'

TASHA: Go where, spirit?

RITA (ELEANOR): 'I was young and pretty and fair prey, I guess—I said I'm not going to go there—'

TASHA: I think you can hear me, can't you? Ellie, we're having a conversation, aren't we?

RITA (ELEANOR): 'Because I don't know who to blame, if indeed someone or something is what I should be looking for—I'm not going there. Now would be the time to speak out I suppose. But—It was all so long ago. I'm not going to go there.'

TASHA: I'm all for exposing secrets in my art. Art is a lie that tells the truth. I believe art is therapy for the artist and the viewer. If you've been abused, or exploited, it's never too late to speak out.

RITA (ELEANOR): 'Rita might now think it was demeaning to her sex, but I didn't then, I just didn't think about... In fact, if I'm honest, being photographed naked, I didn't think I was being objectified, I didn't think of myself as a commodity. No, I felt what every woman wants... I think, to feel desired... I didn't imagine the effect it would have—or did I? —I don't know. I just did what I was told. I think people are so lucky if they know what they're doing.'

TASHA: Yeah. Should I be an artist when no one seems to show the slightest interest in what I do? And I need to earn to live?

RITA (ELEANOR): 'To do what you've not been allowed to do, isn't always an act of liberation, you know. It can trap you.'

TASHA takes the shoes off RITA (ELEANOR).

TASHA: What are you saying? Great artists are liberated by breaking with tradition. You're saying that can be a trap? I don't understand.

ELEANOR: I think what Rita's getting at—

TASHA: Was she called Rita?

ELEANOR: —is that there's no point in just doing something different for the sake of it. If you're going to be an artist, know 'why' and what it is you're trying to do.

TASHA: Well, obviously.

ELEANOR: Clearly someone who didn't like herself because she was never in control of what she did. Did you know her? What did she do? Marry an accountant, bring up four kids and join The Samaritans?

TASHA: You bitch! If she's one of Mum's friends, I never met her.

TASHA picks up MS. YEWTREE's skirt again.

MS. YEWTREE (TASHA): 'Every woman should have a degree.'

ELEANOR: I quite agree, Ms. Yewtree, but I've more letters after my name than a Vice Chancellor and none qualify me to take the life decisions now expected of me.

MS. TEWTREE (TASHA): 'Every woman should make the most of her abilities.'

ELEANOR: I've done that.

MS. TEWTREE (TASHA): 'Ever heard of the remarkable Lena Walker? 1864-1934. Mixed race, daughter of a slave, became a teacher, established a newspaper and founded a bank.'

ELEANOR: Did she have kids?

MS. TEWTREE (TASHA): 'Three. Everything she did demonstrated her consciousness of oppression and her dedication to challenge racial and gender injustice.'

ELEANOR: Could you let her spirit know? If she isn't too busy, I'd really appreciate a visit—

MS. TEWTREE (TASHA): 'She's busy, always busy. There's a two-year waiting list to consult with her, although her holidays on the periphery of the universe are getting longer. I'll ask.'

ELEANOR: Thank you.

TASHA: Oh, my God, Eleanor, you're so clairvoyant!

ELEANOR picks up an apron. She hands the bottle to TASHA.

I'm sure one glass isn't going to affect your baby's health.

MAMA PAPAYA (ELEANOR): (*Calling*) 'Cou cou and flying fish!'

TASHA: Oh hiya Mama Papaya! Hiya! We haven't seen you for ages. Only yesterday Mum was saying 'I wonder what's happened to Mama Papaya?!'

MAMA PAPAYA (ELEANOR): 'I sold Bahama Breezes to MacNellies, flew back home and promptly died. Stroke. I'm sorry I meant to tell your mother. Perhaps you could let her know?'

TASHA: Of course. I'm so sorry. She adored your company.

MAMA PAPAYA (ELEANOR): 'I did everything a good businesswoman should do. Women are the best at business, you know. They're more honest, they're better collaborators, they're better multi-taskers, they guard their profits and they're more resilient. I worked more hours than there were in a day. I created an insatiable demand for delicious Bajan food. But I let my health and my family go. It was the stress.'

TASHA: Mum thinks the only way I'll be financially independent as an artist is if I set up my own business selling sentimental cards and jewellery made out of found objects and polymer clay. My friend Ellie's the entrepreneur, I'll let her know what it takes to be a successful businesswoman, if she hasn't already heard. Did you ever have kids?

MAMA PAPAYA (ELEANOR): 'No.'

ELEANOR: (*Taking off her apron*) Thank you, Mama Papaya.

TASHA: More wine!

TASHA drinks and returns to MRS TEWTREE's skirt. TASHA and ELEANOR talk at each other.

MS. YEWTREE (TASHA): 'It's a fantastic feeling, winning a well-presented argument. Although one mustn't let argument triumph over justice.'

ELEANOR: Yeah.

ELEANOR, desperately looking for a new spirit, picks up her future outfit.

MS. YEWTREE (TASHA): 'I was once told by my professor that I thought more like man than any woman he had ever taught. And, from that discriminatory compliment, I decided I was going to concentrate on gender, human rights and conflict resolution. The dress code remains discriminatory. It does. Totally, discriminatory.'

ELEANOR: Yeah. Yeah. (*Dressed now channelling the future*) 'That's brilliant. I come from a long line of women who stayed at home to look after their families. My Mum was supposed to break with tradition by immigrating, but that didn't work, despite having a brilliant degree. I swore I'd never change my career for a man. I'd pull away before getting too close. Don't get me wrong, I love being in love. I love being wooed, getting flowers and fancy dinners. I never had kids.'

TASHA: Shit! Are you—you are? The future you.

ELEANOR: 'I'm CEO of a sustainable, successful global fashion business.'

TASHA: Congratulations! What's the business called?

ELEANOR: 'Subsequent. Designing out of waste?'

TASHA: When did you become CEO?

ELEANOR: '28.'

TASHA: Umm.

The door buzzer rings. TASHA presses the button on the intercom.

TASHA: Hi Mum—I thought you were going to call—nothing—yeah sure—give us five—three—two—one! Okay I'll let you in, in—I don't know why you haven't got your key—I haven't got it! —We're not drunk, you are!

ELEANOR and TASHA clear up the space as fast as they can re-bagging the clothes. TASHA suddenly stops picks up her future costume.

TASHA: (*Channelling the future TASHA to the audience as though they were guests at a gallery. First Show*). 'Yeah, it's great! It's great to see you all here tonight! It wasn't always the case but now I pick up a brush whenever I feel the muse. For a long time I didn't even try. I think human beings are all animals in disguise and I want to unveil the purest of my, I mean our, desires. No labels. No judgements. Pure expression. I paint what I can't say in words.

The buzzer goes again.

But what I would like to say to you tonight, and I know I'm one of the lucky ones, but the discrepancy between what a woman can make from her art and what a man can is still shameful. We still need more women collectors and directors of big museums. We still need more women patrons. We still need to rewrite art history and show there have always been great female artists who should never have been erased. Go and enjoy my work, share the secrets of our intimate lives right here, right now, tonight!'

ELEANOR: Where were you exhibiting?

TASHA: Popova's.

The buzzer goes again.

ELEANOR: Where's that?

TASHA: Woolwich. We're going to be all right then.

ELEANOR: Life's going to be fine.

TASHA presses the button on the intercom.

TASHA: Now remember, I'm not drunk. Mum, you'll never guess who's dead... Mama Papaya!

THE END

WIDOWED

RUBY is driving, PEARL in the passenger seat. They haven't left yet.

RUBY: We don't have to go?

PEARL: We do.

RUBY: Well, put your belt on.

PEARL obliges.

Wouldn't you rather I told her?

PEARL: No.

RUBY: To give her some time to get used to the idea... time to let it sink in?

RUBY starts the car, and they drive off.

SAT NAV: *In twenty yards turn left into Christchurch Street East. Then take the third exit at the roundabout onto Portway, for the A362.*

RUBY: Mum's so much happier, isn't she?

PEARL: Yes.

RUBY: Now her alcoholic, self-obsessed husband has died.

PEARL: Hey, steady, that's Dad you're talking about.

RUBY: I don't know how she put up with him for so long.

PEARL: For our sake.

RUBY: It was horrible to witness. I left as soon as I could. It was different for you. You were his favourite.

PEARL: That's not true, Ruby.

RUBY: He never forgot your birthday.

SAT NAV: *Take the third exit onto A362.*

RUBY: She's through grieving. She's chopped up his walking stick for kindling.

Pause.

PEARL: I never liked the way Dad just seemed to ignore Mum.

RUBY: Or put her down in public. I mean I know she can be a bit annoying, and doesn't always know what she's talking about, but who does? Did you ever once hear him tell her he loved her, or catch them holding hands?

SAT NAV: *After half a mile, at the roundabout, take the first exit onto Warminster Road A362.*

RUBY: Mum told me the other day that, at last, she felt she'd found herself.

PEARL: Meaning?

RUBY: She said she thought she'd been playing someone else all her life. She'd been a conscientious schoolgirl, sexy teenager, clever student, blushing bride, trophy wife and passable mother. She doesn't want to do what's expected of her anymore.

PEARL: She wants to be more than a widow, doesn't she? She's wants to be a thriving independent woman with new interests of her own.

RUBY: Good for her, I say.

PEARL: Are you sure you're going the right way?

RUBY: I know you don't trust sat nav but we're not getting the map out.

Beat.

PEARL: I don't want to ruin her re-emergence. I hear that's what she calls retirement.

RUBY: I think she's found love again.

PEARL: What?

RUBY: No, I'm serious. Maybe not 'again,' maybe for the 'first time.' She won't talk about it. But she's changed her screen saver, her phone's always engaged, and there are loads flowers in the kitchen.

PEARL: We carry on the A362.

RUBY: I know.

SAT NAV: *In half a mile turn left onto the A362.*

RUBY: She's never been into exercise, but she's started Pilates. 'For her balance,' she says. She's ditched the wine, started eating healthily and says she's never slept better. She's accepted, sort of, that the wrinkles and the reading glasses are here to stay, and the dilated blood vessels in her cheeks and on her legs aren't going anywhere. And she doesn't care. I'm not sure when I'm her age I'll be so accepting.

PEARL: If you get there.

RUBY: I'm sorry. The great thing is she's determined to live each day as though it were her last and have fun.

PEARL: Yes.

RUBY: No different I suppose from knowing when you're going to die.

PEARL: Quite different.

Beat.

RUBY: I'm sorry. I'm so sorry. I'm sorry.

PEARL: It doesn't matter.

SAT NAV: *Turn left!*

RUBY: The one thing she's taught me since Dad died is that the most important relationship you can ever have is the one you have with yourself.

SAT NAV: *Then, at the roundabout, take the first exit onto the A362.*

RUBY: Have you heard Mum's latest?

PEARL: What's she done?

RUBY: As if Pilates, swimming, history of art classes and learning how to cook Peruvian weren't enough, she's joined a spiritualist church.

PEARL: You're kidding me. Why?

RUBY: No she has. I don't know why. She said there was this guy in the market, with blue robin-egg eyes, who sold her a bottle of petiole which reminded her of being a teenager, and then invited her to a spiritualist church where she spoke to Gran.

PEARL: And what did Gran say?

RUBY: 'The feathers make the bird.'

SAT NAV: *At the roundabout, take the third exit onto the A36.*

PEARL: I don't want her searching the net, chucking hope at me like confetti. Treatment to manage the pain is all I want, and the doctors can give me that.

Beat.

RUBY: *(Upset)* Are you okay? Do you want me to stop?

PEARL: I'm fine. Are you?

RUBY: Yeah... No. Sad. Honestly, I'm unbelievably sad. That you're going to die and there are so many things that you might still want to do... but you can't... and you won't see the kids grow up... and—

PEARL: Careful! You nearly ran over that cat.

RUBY: Sorry.

PEARL: It was a black one. A black cat crosses your path, lucky or unlucky?

RUBY: Unlucky. Although a German friend of mine said it depended from which direction. Left to right or right to left?

PEARL: Left to right.

RUBY: Unlucky.

SAT NAV: *In 1.3 Miles, take the second exit onto the A36.*

PEARL: She's going to wonder why we're both coming down—

RUBY: She did ask, and I told her it was a surprise.

PEARL: I know what I'm going to say. I think I'm just going say, 'Mum I've got a brain tumour and they've given me six months. I don't want you to worry because there's nothing that can be done. Let's have a cup of tea and listen to some music.'

RUBY: What music?

PEARL: Bach's Air on a G String.

Bach's Air on G string seeps into the space.

RUBY: *(Close to tears, then crying)* That's sad. That's really sad. That's made me so sad. I'm so sad for you... and I'm sad for the way she's going to react... I mean no parent wants their child to die before they do.

PEARL: Will you please stop crying or neither of us is going to live to tell her what's happened to me!

SAT NAV: *Take the second exit onto the A36.*

The music cuts to something contemporary.

THE END

<u>CHILDISHNESS AND MERE</u>
<u>OBLIVION</u>

CHENISE and SAFEENA are acting students, with a full dressing-up box, and perhaps a toolbox of makeup. They transform themselves into two old women during the scene.

CHENISE: I hate improv, but if we're gonna have to present tomorrow we'd better get on with it.

SAFEENA: I don't mind playing older parts, but how old is old?

CHENISE: (*Reading off a piece of paper*) 'Near death,' it says.

SAFEENA: And do we have to die?

CHENISE: That's a character choice.

SAFEENA: And do they know they're going to die?

CHENISE: Everybody knows they're dying from the moment they're born.

SAFEENA: Obviously, but you know what I mean. What about if I've got a terminal illness and looking for someone to help me die? What about if I ask you, because my quality of life is nonexistent, as a close friend, if you'd be kind enough to place that cushion on my face, the one with the ladybirds on it, and hold it there until I stop breathing... would you?

CHENISE: Euthanasia's been done to death. Let's pretend we have dementia.

SAFEENA: Not everybody gets dementia.

CHENISE: It's on the rise. It'll be easier because we can say what we like.

SAFEENA: That's because everyone's living longer. What's the average age women die? 80? 85?

CHENISE: I know this.

SAFEENA: In this country?

CHENISE: Don't ask me why I know this, or how I know this, but I know this for a fact. 89.

SAFEENA: I'm going to be 90 then.

CHENISE: With dementia?

SAFEENA: Dementia presents differently in different people.

CHENISE: I'm going to be slightly younger than you but I'm not going to tell you how old. What do you know about dementia?

SAFEENA: My Granny has it.

CHENISE: Fab!

SAFEENA: She blames the lead pipes in the house she grew up in.

CHENISE: My Gran's is hereditary.

SAFEENA: So, we can both draw on personal experience. Has she had the tests?

CHENISE: My Gran? Yeah, but because she can count backwards from a hundred in multiples of seven, she's fine, according to the specialists. She was a data analyst and always good at maths. It doesn't seem to matter that she can't remember where she put her diary when it's lying in her lap. So, what's the relationship between us? Let's say, we've known each other for a long time. We're sisters? No, no, no we've played sisters—

SAFEENA: Twice.

CHENISE: Old school friends? Done that. Professional friends? Strangers?

SAFEENA: I don't know... I don't know. Let's just see what happens.

CHENISE: I'm going to forget stuff, but I'd like people not to know whether I'm pretending or actually forgetting.

SAFEENA: I think it's crazy that people put such store in memory. We couldn't cope if we remembered everything. It's important to forget.

CHENISE: It must be horrible though, to start repeating mistakes without realizing it.

SAFEENA: Not if you don't know you're doing it.

CHENISE: It's really hard not to lose patience with Gran.

SAFEENA: My Mum says, 'Go with the flow. It's Granny's second childhood. You'll be there one day.'

CHENISE: So, are you ready? Remember, we've got to be clear about who we are, where we are, when we are, and what's happening.

SAFEENA: Difficult with dementia.

CHENISE: Ha, ha! The characters have dementia, we don't. What's the inciting incident?

SAFEENA: If we try and answer those questions now, we'll never get started.

CHENISE: Ok, I'll emerge in response to whoever you are. Ready?

Pause as they assume an elderly stance.

SAFEENA: Where's my diary?

CHENISE: Hang on a sec. It's my Gran that has the diary. She's my stimulus character.

SAFEENA: Why can't my old person have a diary?

CHENISE: Is that a question Safeena to Chenise? Or a question in character?

SAFEENA: My character has difficulty remembering what day it is without her diary.

CHENISE: I was going to do that.

SAFEENA: Well, you do it.

CHENISE: No, no it doesn't matter. I'll think of something but don't nick all my ideas. Get on with it.

SAFEENA: Honestly, we can both have diaries.

CHENISE: There's something the matter with my breathing.

SAFEENA: You don't smoke.

CHENISE: My husband did. Camel.

SAFEENA: Then you're not who I thought you were.

CHENISE: I'm Flo.

SAFEENA: It'd be fun if you never married but I had had three husbands.

CHENISE: Why?

SAFEENA: Pass me the diary and I'll tell you exactly how old you're going to be on your next birthday.

CHENISE: Budgie, don't you dare!

SAFEENA: Budgie? Who's Budgie?

CHENISE: You're Budgie.

SAFEENA: Can't I choose my own name?

CHENISE: No one gets choose their nickname.

SAFEENA: Except you.

CHENISE: You must be pretty far gone if you can't remember why you're called Budgie.

SAFEENA: I'm not.

CHENISE: Once upon a time, you were small and chirpy.

SAFEENA: That's a lie. I was fat. Ashanti used to call me Queen of the Fatties.

CHENISE: I'm going to call you Budgie.

SAFEENA: And I was never chirpy. I was serious. Serious people don't chirp. Where's my diary? What's the plan?

CHENISE: As soon as I find my glasses, we're going to read this morning's obituaries!

SAFEENA: I'm not deaf, Chenise.

CHENISE: Stay in character, Safeena!

SAFEENA: Look Budgie—

CHENISE: I'm not Budgie. You're Budgie, I'm Flo. Short for Florence. Think Nightingale. Think nurse with the lamp, and a lot of soldiers in field hospitals with bandaged legs all pullied up.

SAFEENA: What day is it?

CHENISE: You've got the fucking diary.

SAFEENA: What's the plan, Budgie?

CHENISE: You're Budgie, Safeena. I'm.... Who am I?

SAFEENA: Chenise.

CHENISE: Flo! Try and remember. Think lady with the lamp.

SAFEENA: What's the plan?

CHENISE: We'll never pass if we can't even remember who we are.

SAFEENA: But isn't that what happens in severe cases of dementia?

CHENISE: I can't remember.

SAFEENA: Would you be so good as to hand me my diary, Flo?

CHENISE: You're holding it, Sparrow—

SAFEENA: Not Sparrow, Cherry!

CHENISE: Not Cherry, Flo! Budgie!

SAFEENA: Short for?

CHENISE: Budgie, look let's forget about the problem some old people have remembering names and who they are. (*Looking at the piece of paper*) It says here improvisation to be between 3-5 minutes, and no longer than ten minutes. That doesn't make sense. Let's say Flo and Budgie pass the day watching Midsomer Murders and reading obituaries... (*Flicking through a newspaper*)

SAFEENA: (*Inspecting her hands*) These aren't my hands.

CHENISE: My fingers look like cheese straws.

SAFEENA: Arthritis.

CHENISE: Who ran over her on her bicycle?

SAFEENA: You can touch me wherever you like.

CHENISE: Act your age not your shoe size!

SAFEENA: Do you think it'd be interesting if we'd once been lovers?

CHENISE: No.

SAFEENA: My favourite song is Bobby Darin's version of Mack the Knife.

CHENISE: I'm happy to explore the fact that we might have shared the same lover, but not that we were lovers. (*Referring to the paper*) I thought the obituaries were always at the back.

SAFEENA: I once had a boyfriend who raped my younger sister.

CHENISE: When?

SAFEENA: My nose dribbles after I've eaten. Does yours do that?

CHENISE: Senile sinuses.

SAFEENA: Where's my diary?

CHENISE: My chest's really hurting.

SAFEENA: (*Consulting her diary*) What's the plan?

CHENISE: (*Still looking for the obituaries*) Whenever I pick up a newspaper, I ask myself, 'is the world getting better or worse?'

SAFEENA: Is there a plan?

CHENISE: There's always lots of famous people dying at this time of year.

SAFEENA: Most of my friends have passed.

CHENISE: When did you last have a bath? (*Reading from the newspaper*) Oh look, Ruth Dhakar's died. The climate one.

SAFEENA: Is the climate getting worse or do I need new shoes?

CHENISE: (*Reading*) 'A permanent memorial is to be created as a lasting tribute to a popular teacher and peace activist Ruth Dhakar.'

SAFEENA: Is it lunchtime?

CHENISE: We've only just had breakfast.

SAFEENA: The fridge is full.

CHENISE: Of your washing.

SAFEENA: Do we need more eggs, Budgie?

CHENISE: Flo! No. (*Gripping her side*) Oiw!

SAFEENA: Are you ready?

CHENISE: Read this for me. I can't find my glasses.

SAFEENA: (*Reading the obituary*) 'She was a useful person who was committed to saving the planet.'

CHENISE: The thing about obituaries is when you have to cram a life into five hundred words, people always appear more successful and nicer than they actually were.

SAFEENA: Shall we go to the funeral?

CHENISE: When is it?

SAFEENA: 30th of October.

CHENISE: Put it in the diary.

SAFEENA: (*Finding the entry in the diary*) Oh, look. It's already here.

CHENISE: Oh, look. This is an old paper.

SAFEENA: They're bound to play 'when the saints.'

CHENISE: (*About the paper*) What does it matter what it says in the paper. The news just repeats itself.

SAFEENA: (*Starts singing*)

Oh, when the saints go marchin' in
Oh, when the saints go marchin' in,

CHENISE & SAFEENA:

Lord, how I want to be in that number

When the saints go marchin' in!

CHENISE: Finish crossword?

CHENISE hands SAFEENA the crossword.

SAFEENA: (*Reading a clue*) 'Occasion for spirited conversation...'

CHENISE: Piss up.

SAFEENA: Seance.

CHENISE: Seance. Oiw! What's happening to me. My arms feel, all tingly.

SAFEENA: (*Reading crossword clue*) 'Lady dines out? That's unforgivable!' (*Reading another*) 'End of the world. 8 letters.' North Pole.

CHENISE: That's 9. Doomsday. Deadly sin.

SAFEENA: Ragnarok. That's 8. And it fits with 11 across. Let's try 23 down.

CHENISE: I hate crosswords.

CHENISE: My chest.

SAFEENA: Where've you put my lavender water?

CHENISE: (*Breathless*) Budgie, I think I'm having a... Where have you put the phone? Please Budgie. I'm being serious. This is an emergency!

CHENISE loses consciousness.

SAFEENA: I'm sorry but I'm not having you phone the doctor. I never put the milk in oven, went shopping in my dressing gown, stole the ginger biscuits or stripped in Smiths. Let's end it there. Phew! That was crazy. Chenise? Chenise! Why are you lying on the floor? Get up. Let's try it again. Get up, Chenise. We present tomorrow.

Silence.

SAFEENA leans forward to check that CHENISE is breathing.

SAFEENA: (*Quietly*) Chenise? This isn't fair. Chenise? Please don't tell me—How do I know? Help! Help! (*To the audience*) Is there a doctor in the house?

As SAFEENA moves forward, CHENISE gets up behind her, immediately, smiling.

CHENISE: I was only acting.

SAFEENA: That's not funny. Don't ever do that again!

CHENISE: You thought I was really dead?

SAFEENA: Let's try it tomorrow and see what the others think.

THE END

CURTAIN

www.ingramcontent.com/pod-product-compliance
Lightning Source LLC
Chambersburg PA
CBHW072103110526
44590CB00018B/3298